Older Adulthood

Older Adulthood
Learning Activities for Understanding Aging

by

Stephen Fried, Ph.D.
Professor and Chair
Department of Psychology
Park College
Parkville, Missouri

Dorothy Van Booven, R.N., M.A.
Senior Associate
Arthur Clark Associates
Kansas City, Missouri

and

Cindy MacQuarrie, M.N., R.N.C.
Clinical Programs Manager
Arthur Clark Associates
Kansas City, Missouri

HEALTH PROFESSIONS PRESS

Baltimore • London • Toronto • Sydney

Health Professions Press, Inc.
P.O. Box 10624
Baltimore, Maryland 21285-0624

Typeset by Brushwood Graphics, Inc., Baltimore, Maryland.
Manufactured in the United States of America by
The Maple Press Company, York, Pennsylvania.

Library of Congress Cataloging-in-Publication Data
Fried, Stephen.
  Older adulthood: learning activities for understanding aging/by
Stephen Fried and Dorothy Van Booven, and Cindy MacQuarrie.
    p.   cm.
  Includes bibliographical references and index.
  ISBN 1-878812-10-6 :
  1. Aging—Study and teaching—United States. 2. Aged—Ser-
vices for—Study and teaching—United States. 3. Aged—United
States—Psychology. I. Van Booven, Dorothy. II. MacQuarrie,
Cindy. III. Title.
  [DNLM: 1. Aging—physiology. 2. Aging—psychology.
3. Geriatrics—education—United States. 4. Health Services for the
Aged—United States.   WT 104 F899o]
HQ1064.U5F75   1993
305.26'07'073—dc20
DNLM/DLC
for Library of Congress   92-1560
                                                                                CIP
British Library Cataloguing-in-Publication data are available from
the British Library.

Contents

Foreword by *Sister Rose Therese Bahr*.. ix
About the Authors vii
Acknowledgments xi

Introduction   Teaching Activities for the Study of Gerontology 1

Chapter 1   Perceptions of Aging 5
    Knowledge of Older Adults Quiz... 9
    When Is a Person Old? 13
    What Will I Be Like When I Am 75? 16
    Age Norming 19
    Is Your Social Clock Ticking? 23
    The Decade Game... 26

Chapter 2   Stereotyping and Ageism 29
    The Aging Stereotype Game 33
    Happy Birthday—Another Year! 37
    Older Adults and Television 40
    Myths About Aging... 42

Chapter 3   Physical Aging.. 45
    Knowledge of Physical Aging Quiz... 49
    Dietary Changes: A Meal Planning Strategy 52
    Ease or Dis-ease: Physical Access to Health Care... 60
    When Physical Function Is Limited.. 64
    Knowledge of Alzheimer's Disease Quiz 68

Chapter 4   Psychological Aging... 71
    The Timeline Interview 75
    Maintaining Independence... 78
    Fear of Falling 82
    Alcoholism in Later Life 86

Chapter 5   Sexuality and Aging 91
    Knowledge of Sexuality and Aging Quiz... 95
    Sexuality and the Older Adult 99
    The Empty Bed 102

Chapter 6   Family Issues in Aging..105
    The Generation Gap Rap..108
    Adult Children and Their Parents...111
    The Role of Grandparents: The Ideal Versus the Real...114
    Loss and Widowhood 117
    Far From Home 120

Chapter 7 Maximizing Choices...125
    Congratulations, You're Retired! 129
    Balancing the Fixed Income Budget..133
    Developing a Political Platform for Older Americans 137
    A Way to Spend My Days 140

Chapter 8 Moving to a Long-Term Care Facility 145
    Welcome to Our Nursing Home: Facilitating Adjustment 148
    Applying the Resident's Bill of Rights 152
    A Case of Abuse 159
    The Ideal Nursing Home..164

Chapter 9 Death and Dying...167
    Contemplating Endings 169
    Dealing with Death 172
    Grieving and Surviving..174
    The Ethics of Dying...178

Chapter 10 Issues for Professional Caregivers...183
    Working with a Problem Family Member...187
    Stress Management for the Professional Caregiver....................................191
    The Case of the Caring Professional...194

Appendix A Evaluating the Effectiveness of Learning Activities 197

Appendix B Answer Key 199

Annotated Bibliography 211

About the Authors

Stephen Fried, Ph.D., Department of Psychology, Park College, Parkville, Missouri 64152. Dr. Fried is Professor and Chair of the Department of Psychology, Park College, in Parkville, Missouri. In addition to teaching both undergraduate and graduate students, he has taught staff management in hospitals, nursing homes, and industry. He consults in staff development, team building, employee attitude surveys, management coaching, and conflict resolution.

Dorothy Van Booven, R.N., M.A., Arthur Clark Associates, Inc., 2900 Rockcreek Parkway, Suite 420, North Kansas City, Missouri 64117. Ms. Van Booven is Senior Associate with Arthur Clark Associates, a health care planning and market development firm that provides a comprehensive range of consultive services to all types of health care professionals and providers. Ms. Van Booven has over 25 years of professional experience in nursing, teaching, management, and program development.

Cindy MacQuarrie, M.N., R.N.C., Arthur Clark Associates, Inc., 2900 Rockcreek Parkway, Suite 420, North Kansas City, Missouri 64117. Ms. MacQuarrie is Clinical Programs Manager with Arthur Clark Associates. She has taught gerontology at colleges and in continuing education programs, and has worked with health care organizations to develop programs for older adults.

Foreword

ALTHOUGH AMERICA IS A "GREYING" SOCIETY, MUCH REMAINS TO BE ACCOMPLISHED IN THE area of education for health professionals, family members, and younger people so that they comprehend fully the complexities of the aging process. Many of the myths and stereotypes about older adults that abound contribute to prejudice against older adults and reduce their quality of life. With the vast increase in the number of older adults projected in the United States over the next 50 years, peaking between 2020 and 2030, more and more emphasis on the uniqueness of older adults is required in order to foster an environment that is supportive of this segment of the population. In so doing, the negative images that are currently so prominent may be diminished.

Given this background, it is indeed refreshing to read *Older Adulthood: Learning Activities for Understanding Aging*. The 10 chapters of the book cover the key areas with which students interested in understanding aging need to be familiar. The concepts presented in each chapter are thoroughly explained in the informative introductory material that precedes the learning activities in each chapter. The learning activities themselves represent an invaluable complement to more traditional learning tools, and promise to enrich classes on aging.

Older adults of the future will be better educated and more sophisticated than the older adults of today. The cohorts of the future will be better able to take care of themselves and will consequently have greater expectations of health professionals and society at large. The importance of understanding older adults from a holistic perspective—the physical, psychosocial, and spiritual dimensions—is critical to ensuring the dignity and respect that each older adult should expect from every member of society.

I congratulate the authors for their major contribution to the gerontological and educational literature. My prediction is that this text will be on many reference lists in the United States and throughout the world.

Sister Rose Therese Bahr, A.S.C., Ph.D., R.N., FAAN
Sister Adorers of the Blood of Christ
Wichita, Kansas

Acknowledgments

MANY PEOPLE HAVE HELPED US THROUGH VARIOUS STAGES OF THE DEVELOPMENT OF THIS book. We would like to thank the following persons: Ann Schultis and Betty Vestal, Park College Library; Dr. Ted Albrecht, School of Music, Kent State University; Dr. Mack Winholtz, Department of Sociology, Park College; Dr. Jack Mulligan, Department of Family Practice, University of Missouri—Kansas City; and, Sister Rose Therese Bahr, Sister Adorers of the Blood of Christ, Wichita, Kansas.

Stephen Fried was awarded a Faculty Development Grant from Park College, which aided in the development of many of the learning activities. Support and constructive criticism were provided by Connie Boswell Fried; Katherine, Kim, and Kurt Fried; Theresa, Donna, Mark, and Marla Van Booven; Karen Houchins; Kerianne Tupac; and Dr. Ron MacQuarrie. Various drafts of the manuscript were skillfully typed by Philistia Bronston and Camille Lloyd.

Barbara Karni, our editor, offered much guidance, patience, and stimulation. Barbara is everything an editor should be. The book is definitely much better because of Barbara's skill and persistence.

Earlier versions of five of the learning activities (Knowledge of the Older Adults Quiz, The Aging Stereotype Game, Happy Birthday—Another Year!, Older Adults and Television, and What Will I Be Like When I Am 75?) appeared in "Learning activities for understanding aging," by Stephen Fried. This article was published in 1988 in *Teaching of Psychology, Volume 15*. These activities are used by permission of Lawrence Erlbaum Associates.

It is our hope that students, faculty, and practitioners will gain understanding of older adults and the aging process from the learning activities contained in this book.

We dedicate the book with love and gratitude to our fathers:
Harold Fried (1915–1991),
Francis Speichinger (1920–1991),
J. Kennard Smith (1914–)

Older Adulthood

Introduction

Teaching Activities for the Study of Gerontology

OLDER ADULTHOOD: LEARNING ACTIVITIES FOR UNDERSTANDING AGING IS DE-signed to provide experiential materials that facilitate the understanding of gerontology. Interest in gerontology continues to grow as the number of older adults rises. Students can be taught about the aging process using a wide variety of teaching methods, including lectures, discussion, and activities. This book offers a variety of learning activities, which can be used to augment any or all of the other teaching methodologies.

Over the past 15 years, we have used experiential learning as the basis for much of our teaching. *Older Adulthood: Learning Activities for Understanding Aging* is based on a participatory approach to learning and what we believe to be sound educational practice. Through involvement in the learning process, the learner can develop an understanding of aging in a nonthreatening fashion. This can lead to more positive and accepting attitudes toward aging and toward older adults.

This book of learning activities has been developed for use in college classrooms, in continuing education settings, and in inservice development. Audiences include college students studying sociology, psychology, social work, and the health sciences, including nursing and allied health. Additionally, the learning activities can be used to teach a variety of students in nonacademic settings, including nurses, nursing assistants, nursing home administrators, dietary aides, and other health professionals involved in the care of older adults. Many of the activities have been designed to fulfill the requirements for continuing education for nursing assistants working in nursing homes.

The learning activities can be used for beginning students to provide background about the aging process or in expanding the knowledge of students already familiar with aging. Educators can also benefit from completing the learning activities and investigating the reading described in the annotated bibliographies.

The book has been organized around 10 general themes:

- Perceptions of aging
- Stereotypes and ageism
- Physical aging
- Psychological aging
- Sexuality
- Family issues
- Maximizing choices
- The long-term care facility
- Death and dying
- Issues for professional caregivers

Each chapter begins with an introduction to the topics under study and a brief description of the activities, and includes appropriate learning activities. At the end of the book, the reader is provided with annotated bibliographies to each chapter. Through consulting the bibliography, both educators and students may continue the study of gerontology.

The topical areas covered in *Older Adulthood: Learning Activities for Understanding Aging* include activities that address a wide variety of concepts in gerontology. In Chapter 1, entitled "Perceptions of Aging," demographic information is presented and the student is afforded an opportunity to think about his or her own aging. Chapter 2, "Stereotyping and Ageism," deals with the various myths associated with the aging process and how attitudes toward aging are related to behavior toward older adults. In Chapter 3, "Physical Aging," learners are provided with information on physical changes associated with aging, dietary management, physical access to health care facilities, and Alzheimer's disease. Chapter 4, "Psychological Aging," provides activities on such psychological issues as independence, the fear of falling, and alcoholism. In Chapter 5, "Sexuality and Aging," learners consider the facts about sexuality of older adults, and examine their own perceptions of sexuality. In Chapter 6, "Family Issues in Aging," relationships between adults and their parents are examined, and the roles of grandparenthood and widowhood are considered. In Chapter 7, "Maximizing Choices," learners examine the topics of retirement, budgeting on a fixed income, political concerns, and volunteerism. In Chapter 8, the learner considers "Moving to a Long-Term Care Facility." Activities in this chapter cover moving to a nursing home, resident rights, elder abuse, and the "ideal" nursing facility. Chapter 9, "Death and Dying," considers changes that accompany perceptions of death over the life cycle, grieving, surviving, and ethical issues. Finally, Chapter 10, "Issues for Professional Caregivers," examines such issues as dealing with a problem family member, burnout, and stress management.

The activities found in this text are most successful when used in conjunction with a teaching style that reflects principles of adult learning. A supportive teaching style encourages learners to be an effective resource. Learners have many reasons for engaging in coursework or continuing education classes in gerontology, and an effective teacher considers the differing interests and needs of learners.

Each activity is introduced with a standard format that includes the following components:

- **Purpose** Provides the educator with an understanding of the overall nature of the activity and lists objectives that the learner is expected to meet after completing the activity.

- **Time Required** Indicates a suggested time frame required to complete the activity and discuss it in class. Additional time may be needed for a lecture presentation of the material under consideration. These time frames are based on the experience of the authors and may vary across learners and educators.

- **Procedure** Lists the specific steps involved to complete the activity. The educator may wish to copy the instructions for learners to use in preparation for an activity.

- **Discussion Questions** Serve as a springboard for class discussion after the learning activity has been completed. These questions may help to encourage participation and critical thinking, and are designed to facilitate the learning process.

Instructors are advised to review each learning activity prior to using it in a classroom or workshop setting. Where activities contain concepts that are unfamiliar to some learners, instructors may want to present a lecture or assign reading material prior to using the teaching activity in this book.

Some learners may be especially sensitive to a particular topic. For example, learners who have recently experienced the death of a loved one may have difficulty with the activities on death and dying. As much as possible, instructors should make an effort to be cognizant of the special needs of learners.

The answer key at the end of the book includes answers to all of the quizzes and some of the learning activities contained in the book. Because some of the learning activities require individual responses, answers to many of the activities are not included. At the end of the book, an evaluation instrument is included that can be used to determine the effectiveness of the activities as learning tools. We have found that the evaluation of an activity provides useful feedback in helping the instructor decide to change the content of or amount of time alotted to a particular learning experience.

The authors believe that this text offers opportunities to facilitate the learning and teaching of gerontology. We wish you much success in your teaching and learning endeavors.

Chapter 1

Perceptions of Aging

WE BEGIN OUR STUDY OF GERONTOLOGY BY EXAMINING DEMOGRAPHIC DATA. Our perceptions of older adults and of the aging process are influenced to some extent by the characteristics of the older people with whom we come in contact, yet our direct experience is limited to a small sample of the larger population of older adults.

Approximately one in eight Americans is 65 years of age or older. This means that in 1989, 31 million Americans were 65 or older. The percentage of older Americans rose substantially since the turn of the century, increasing from 2.1% of the population in 1900 to 12.5% in 1989. As of 1989, there were about 145 women 65 and over for every 100 older men. The number of older adults will continue to grow. However, the rate of growth of the older population is expected to slow down in the 1990s due to the small number of births during the Great Depression. Rapid growth in the older population is anticipated between the years 2010 and 2030 as the "baby boomers" reach old age. By the year 2030, there are expected to be approximately 66 million Americans 65 or older, representing over 20% of the population.

As of 1991, only 5% of the older population were living in nursing homes. This figure rose substantially with age, however, with about 22% of people over 85 years old residing in institutional settings. In 1984, about 40% of older women and 15% of older men lived alone. Eighty percent of older adults had living children. About two-thirds of these people lived within 30 minutes driving time of an adult child, more than 6 of 10 visited weekly with a child, and about three-fourths engaged in telephone conversations with their children at least once a week.

In 1990, the median income for men 65 and over was just over $14,100; for older women, the figure was about $8,000. The poverty rate

Demographic data in this chapter are from *Current Population Reports* (Washington, DC: Government Printing Office, 1989), *Aging in the 80s* (Hyattsville, MD: Center for Health Statistics, 1990), and *State Population and Household Estimates, 1980–1988* (Washington, DC: U.S. Department of Commerce Bureau of the Census).

for older women was almost twice that of older men (14% compared to 8%). Poverty rates differ markedly by race and ethnicity: while one in 10 whites 65 and over lives below the poverty line, one in five older Hispanics and one in three older African-Americans are impoverished.

The important sources of income for older adults are Social Security, asset income, earnings, and pensions. In 1989, older adults represented almost 3% of the labor force and about half of all older workers were employed on a part-time basis.

The educational level of the older population is increasing steadily. The median level of education increased from 8.7 years in 1970 to 12.1 years in 1988. In addition, during those same years, the percentage of people who completed high school went from 28% to 54%. By 1988, 11% of the older population had completed at least 4 years of college.

The majority of older Americans have at least one health problem. As of 1990, the most frequently occurring health problems among older people were: arthritis, hypertension, hearing impairments, heart disease, cataracts, sinusitis, orthopedic problems, diabetes, and assorted visual impairments. In that same year, older adults accounted for one-third of all stays in hospitals.

Older people are less likely to relocate than younger people. As of 1988, over half of all older adults lived in the nine states of California, New York, Florida, Pennsylvania, Texas, Illinois, Ohio, and Michigan.

Certainly our understanding and perceptions of aging are affected by the assortment of facts about the growing population of older Americans. But perceptions are also affected by the reality of our own aging. The most common indicator of aging of which each individual is reminded with each passing birthday is that of chronological age. Some scholars have criticized chronological age as an indicator of human development on the grounds that each person ages at a different rate, various aspects of an individual may age at different rates, and the particular meaning of a certain number of years may vary at different places in the lifespan. The last point can be illustrated by comparing the changes that occur in the first 2 years of life with those changes that may occur between the ages of 38 and 40 or 68 and 70. Certainly, the first 2 years of life bring many more changes than any other 2-year period.

Biological aging is a result of changes that occur at the genetic level. Numerous theories of biological aging have been suggested, but no theory has been able to explain why people age at different rates. That is, we do not understand why a 70-year-old may show fewer signs of physical aging than a 50-year-old.

An individual's ability to adapt is reflected through psychological age. Here, too, numerous theories have been developed, but no single theory can explain fully why people react to aging as they do. **Functional age** reflects one's ability to live in a society, and entails social, psychological and biological age. An individual's **social age** is described in terms of how closely that person follows what are considered to be age-appropriate norms. Age norms are socially approved behaviors for a particular age group. Every society appears to encourage people to behave in certain ways depending on their respective ages. Age norms may provide what University of Chicago professor Bernice Neugarten calls a "social clock," by which an individual gauges personal progress through life's course. Some events may occur "on-time" (e.g., retiring around the age of 65) and some occurrences may be perceived as "off-time" (e.g., marrying for the first time at the age of 70). The social and psychological meanings of an event may be influenced by its position on the clock relative to other people or to generally understood cultural expectations. There is not necessarily a correct or incorrect time for any life events, but the larger culture does attempt to provide guidelines for people to follow through the lifespan.

American society is aging, which undoubtedly will influence perceptions of aging. Knowledge of aging affects our perceptions of ourselves as well as others. One convenient way of categorizing people is by age, but there are several types of age. Perhaps the least useful of these types of age is that of chronological age, since the number of years since birth tells us very little about an individual. Each of us is influenced by society's age norms and the "social clock" that emerges from those norms.

DESCRIPTION OF ACTIVITIES

Knowledge of Older Adults Quiz

In this 15-item questionnaire, demographic data regarding older adults are addressed. The items in this quiz examine the relative size of the older population, geographic dispersion, gender, race, poverty, marital status, health problems, longevity, frequency of interaction with adult children, and future growth of the population of elderly persons.

When Is a Person Old?

This exercise focuses on the various meanings of the terms "old" and "age." Although chronological age is the most common indicator of aging, it is by no means the only one. Learners differentiate among chronological, biological, psychological, and social age, and are asked to consider what it means to be old by these standards. Additionally, learners are asked to examine their own perceptions of being or feeling "old."

What Will I Be Like When I Am 75?

Learners are asked to look into the future and to consider what they might be like at the age of 75. They are asked to make projections regarding possible similarities and differences between the way that they currently view themselves and how they may view themselves at age 75. Learners make judgments about behavior, appearance, physical capacity, and preferences.

Age Norming

In this activity, learners list some of the socially prescribed privileges and obligations associated with a variety of age groups. Age norms may dictate what is "suitable" or "appropriate," and are typically arbitrary, limiting a person to behaving in response to the expectations of others. By listing age normative behaviors, learners examine the pervasiveness of age-grading in the general society, the possible relationship between social roles and self concept, and issues related to adaptation and conflict with social norms.

Is Your Social Clock Ticking?

The concept of the social clock is analyzed through this learning activity. Since most people seem to care how they are viewed by others, age norms can provide a social clock by which the individual gauges personal progress through life. Through group interaction, learners examine several activities in which they have engaged "on time" and "off time." Learners consider the psychological and sociological implications of being behind or ahead of time, and what this means in a society that places great emphasis on adhering to the social clock.

The Decade Game

The Decade Game examines the concepts of cohort effects and values, as applied to historical periods and events. Through small groups, learners explore historical events in relation to values instilled by society. Learners list significant events from a specific decade and several values that were reinforced during that period. Through this activity, learners explore the relationships among historical events, societal values, and individual values.

Activity

Knowledge of Older Adults Quiz

PURPOSE

The purpose of this activity is to test the learner's knowledge of demographic data about older adults. Upon completion of this activity, the learner will be able to:

1. Assess his or her knowledge of the basic demographics of older people.

2. Receive feedback regarding knowledge of older people.

TIME REQUIRED

40 minutes (15 minutes to complete the quiz and 25 minutes to discuss the answers in class)

PROCEDURE

1. Learners take the quiz presented in the activity sheet.

2. The instructor reviews the answers to the quiz in class.

3. The instructor may lead a discussion based on the following questions.

DISCUSSION QUESTIONS

1. Which of the correct answers to the quiz most surprised you? Why?

2. What are some consequences of aging for the health care system?

3. What are some psychological and social implications of the fact that women live longer than men?

4. What is the effect of the higher educational level of older adults today relative to 30 years ago?

5. What do you think life for older people will be like in this country in the mid–twenty-first century? Explain.

Knowledge of Older Adults Quiz

Indicate whether each of the following statements is true or false.

		True	False
1.	In the United States, about one in eight people is 65 years of age or older.	_____	_____
2.	By the year 2030, older adults may represent over one-fifth of the U.S. population.	_____	_____
3.	The growth of the older population will slow down in the 1990s because of the relatively low birth rate during the Great Depression.	_____	_____
4.	A child born in 1988 could expect to live about 75 years.	_____	_____
5.	Median income for older women was over $15,000 in 1990.	_____	_____
6.	The most common health problem among older adults is arthritis.	_____	_____
7.	Thirty percent of all older adults have diabetes.	_____	_____
8.	About 75% of older adults have significant hearing impairments.	_____	_____
9.	There are about 150 older women for every 100 older men.	_____	_____
10.	Older men are twice as likely to be married as are older women.	_____	_____

		True	False
11.	Older men have a higher poverty rate than older women.	_____	_____
12.	Half of all older women are widows.	_____	_____
13.	About one-third of older African-Americans live below the poverty line.	_____	_____
14.	The educational level of the older population has been steadily decreasing.	_____	_____
15.	Most parents over the age of 65 see one of their adult children at least twice a month.	_____	_____

```
┌─────────────────────────────────┐
│         ┌───────────┐           │
│         │ Activity  │           │
│         └───────────┘           │
│                                 │
│    When Is a Person Old?        │
│                                 │
└─────────────────────────────────┘
```

PURPOSE

The purpose of this activity is to prompt the learner to think about various meanings of the term "old." Upon completion of this activity, the learner will be able to:

1. Describe several possible meanings of "old."

2. Define chronological age.

3. Relate the term "old" to physical change.

4. Analyze the term "old" as it relates to social roles.

TIME REQUIRED

1 hour (20 minutes to complete the activity sheet, 20 minutes to discuss responses with partners, and 20 minutes to discuss the activity as a class)

PROCEDURE

1. Learners complete the activity sheet individually.

2. Following completion of the activity sheets, the instructor divides the class into pairs. Learners discuss their responses to the activity sheet with their partners.

3. Following these discussions, the instructor leads a class discussion of the activity.

4. The instructor may lead a more general class discussion based on the following questions.

DISCUSSION QUESTIONS

1. What physical changes often occur with age?

2. Can different parts of the body age at different rates? Explain.

3. How does being "old" relate to life expectancy?

4. How do people define themselves in terms of social roles?

5. How is socialization related to one's feeling "old"?

6. Comment on the expression "You're as old as you feel!"

When Is a Person Old?

Prepare written answers to the following questions. When you and your partner have finished, discuss your responses with each other.

1. When is someone old?

2. What is chronological age?

3. Using chronological age as an indicator, when is someone old?

4. When is someone physically old?

5. What is a social role?

6. Define "old" in terms of two or three social roles.

What Will I Be Like When I Am 75?

PURPOSE

The purpose of this activity is to prompt the learner to consider what he or she will be like as an older adult. Upon completion of this activity, the learner will be able to:

1. Describe him- or herself as a 75-year-old.

2. Describe some of the physiological and psychological changes that occur as people age.

TIME REQUIRED

50 minutes (25 minutes to complete the activity sheet and 25 minutes to discuss the activity in class)

PROCEDURE

1. Learners complete the activity sheet individually.

2. Following completion of the activity sheets, the instructor divides the class into pairs. Learners discuss their responses to the activity sheet with their partners.

3. Following these discussions, the instructor leads a class discussion of the activity.

4. The instructor may lead a more general class discussion based on the following questions.

DISCUSSION QUESTIONS

1. What are some characteristics of physical aging?

2. What are some psychological changes that may accompany aging?

3. Is personality stable or does it change over the lifespan?

4. Are there more differences between 25- and 50-year-olds, or between 50- and 75-year-olds? Explain.

5. What are the positive aspects of being 75? What are the negative aspects?

What Will I Be Like When I Am 75?

Prepare written answers to the following questions. When you and your partner have finished, discuss your responses with each other.

1. Which of your current behaviors will change and which will stay the same when you are 75?

2. In what ways will you look like you do now and in what ways will you look different when you are 75?

3. What do you think your eyesight, hearing, and physical stamina will be like at age 75?

4. What do you expect to enjoy about being 75?

5. What do you expect to miss about not being your present age?

6. Is it difficult to imagine yourself at 75? Why or why not?

Age Norming

PURPOSE

The purpose of this activity is to allow the learner to examine some of the societal norms generally associated with various age groups. Upon completion of this activity, the learner will be able to:

1. Give specific examples of age norms.

2. Identify the two-fold nature of age norms (obligations and privileges).

TIME REQUIRED

45 minutes (20 minutes to complete the activity sheet and 25 minutes to discuss the activity in class)

PROCEDURE

1. Learners complete the activity sheet individually.

2. Following completion of the activity sheets, the instructor divides the class into pairs. Learners discuss their responses to the activity sheet with their partners.

3. Following these discussions, the instructor leads a class discussion of the activity.

4. The instructor may lead a more general class discussion based on the following questions.

DISCUSSION QUESTIONS

1. What is the relationship between one's social roles and one's self-concept?

2. Why does every society attempt to teach its members the social rules peculiar to that society?

3. Is America an age-graded society?

4. Give examples of how older adults might anticipate and adapt to age-related norms.

Age Norming

Complete the activity sheet by providing at least two examples of socially prescribed obligations and privileges for each of the age groups listed below. (As an example, the first age group has been completed.)

Age group	Obligations	Privileges
20–29	*Completing one's education; working full-time; possibly supporting a family*	*Gaining independence from parents; probably living apart from parents*
30–39		
40–49		
50–59		

(continued)

Age group	Obligations	Privileges
60–69		
70 and older		

```
┌─────────────────────┐
│      Activity       │
└─────────────────────┘
```

Is Your Social Clock Ticking?

PURPOSE

The purpose of this activity is to familiarize the learner with the concept of the social clock. Upon completion of this activity, the learner will be able to:

1. Define the term "social clock."

2. Describe several "off-time" and "on-time" events that have occurred in his or her life.

3. Appraise how social clocks influence both behavior and self-concept.

TIME REQUIRED

45 minutes (20 minutes to complete the activity sheet and 25 minutes to discuss the activity in class)

PROCEDURE

1. The class is divided into groups of four or five.

2. Each group completes the activity sheet.

3. Following completion of the activity sheet, each group presents its findings to the entire class.

4. The instructor leads a class discussion of the activity.

5. The instructor may lead a more general discussion based on the following questions.

DISCUSSION QUESTIONS

1. Why does Western culture emphasize engaging in certain behavior "on-time"?

2. Comment on some of the consequences of a society abandoning its social clocks.

3. Have you ever been discouraged from planning or accomplishing a goal "ahead of time"? Explain.

4. Do you expect to follow the social clock for most events in your life? Explain.

Is Your Social Clock Ticking?

Prepare written answers to the following questions.

1. List several goals that you have accomplished "on time."

2. List several goals that you have been working toward "off time."

3. Are there different social clocks based on social class, ethnic group, or gender? Give examples.

4. Why do we sometimes feel compelled to be "on time" according to the social clock?

5. What are some psychological and social costs incurred when we are "off time"?

```
┌─────────────────────────────────────┐
│           ┌──────────┐              │
│           │ Activity │              │
│           └──────────┘              │
│                                     │
│        The Decade Game              │
│                                     │
└─────────────────────────────────────┘
```

PURPOSE

The purpose of this activity is to examine the relationship between significant historical events and culturally promoted values. Upon completion of this activity, the learner will be able to:

1. List some of the most significant events of the 1930s, 1940s, 1950s, 1960s, 1970s, and 1980s.

2. Describe some of the values that were promoted during each decade.

3. Discuss the relationships among historical events, societal values, and individual values.

4. Analyze how events affect the evolution of values.

TIME REQUIRED

1 hour (30 minutes to complete the activity sheet and 30 minutes to discuss the activity in class)

PROCEDURE

1. The class is divided into six groups, each group representing a different decade between the 1930s and the 1980s.

2. Each group completes the activity sheet.

3. After all the groups have completed the activity sheets, each group, beginning with the group representing the 1930s, shares its list with the rest of the class. Learners are encouraged to add to the list as the discussion unfolds.

4. After the group presentations are completed, the instructor leads a class discussion of the activity.

5. The instructor may lead a more general class discussion based on the following questions.

DISCUSSION QUESTIONS

1. What historical events most influenced the development of your values?

2. What historical events most influenced the development of your parents' values?

3. What is the source of our values?

4. What are cohort effects?

5. What values are represented by "baby boomers"?

6. How might the values of the "baby boomers" influence our society in the early twenty-first century?

The Decade Game

For the decade assigned to your group, identify the major historical events and the values and behaviors that were encouraged during that decade.

Important historical events of the 19__s	Promoted values and behaviors of the 19__s

Chapter 2

Stereotyping and Ageism

IN THIS CHAPTER, STEREOTYPES REGARDING OLDER ADULTS ARE EXPLORED. According to gerontologist Georgia Barrow, "Stereotypes are generalized beliefs or opinions produced by irrational thinking."[1] Stereotypes are used to organize and structure perceptions of the world. Since stereotypes fail to account for individual differences, they are inadequate. Even though stereotypes are irrational, such beliefs can be reinforced through experience. For example, suppose that an individual works in a long-term care facility where residents display significant physical disabilities. From this on-going contact with frail older adults, one might become inclined to stereotype all older people as having disabilities.

Stereotyping of older adults is a reflection of ageism, much as sexist stereotyping of women reflects sexism and racial stereotyping reflects racism. Ageism, a term coined by geriatrician/gerontologist Robert Butler, refers to "the prejudices and stereotypes that are applied to older people sheerly on the basis of their age."[2] In describing the roots of ageism, Butler argues that ageism is based upon several social myths. For example, classifying all older adults according to their chronological age is a form of ageism, since there is great variability in aging between and within people. Some people appear to be "younger" or "older" than others who were born the same year. Each person has bodily systems that seem to be more or less resilient or healthy than others. In addition, Butler suggests that we perpetuate myths of inflexibility, senility, lack of productivity, disengagement, and even serenity about older adults.

Philosopher Joseph Esposito believes that the myths and stereotypes associated with ageism give rise to a kind of paternalism. Paternalism implies that those toward whom we feel paternalistic are somehow inferior to us. A particularly disturbing form of paternalism is reflected in what

---

[1]Barrow, G. (1989). *Aging, the individual, and society* (4th ed.). St. Paul: West Publishing Co., p. 25.

[2]Butler, R., Lewis, M., & Sunderland, T. (1991). *Aging and mental health: Positive psychosocial and biomedical approaches* (4th ed.). New York: MacMillan, p. 243.

sociologists Arnold Arluke and Jack Levin call "infantilization." According to Arluke and Levin, infantilization characterizes old age as a second childhood and operates to keep older adults in their place. Referring to older people as children may, in effect, be similar to the nineteenth century slaveholder's labeling of an African-American adult as a "boy."

Ageism is deeply rooted in the English language. Using a number of sources, including the *Oxford English Dictionary,* sociologist Herbert Covey traced words used to describe older adults. One of the critical factors in understanding the history of this terminology appears to be that of gender. Words used to describe older men center on their being conservative, eccentric, feeble, incompetent, narrow-minded, old-fashioned, stingy, stupid, or uncouth. Words referring to older women suggest bad temper, bossiness, disagreeableness, mysticism, repulsiveness, spinsterhood, spitefulness, and unattractiveness. Animal-related terms have also been used to describe older people. Men have been called "old buzzard" or "old goat," while women have been referred to as "old bird" or "old trout." One essential difference in the terminology of old age is that often women are deemed to be "old" at an earlier age than are men. In this way, sexism has joined ageism in the use of the English language.

Stereotyping and ageism are reflected in humor. Sociologist Erdman Palmore believes that many jokes about older adults reveal a negative view of the aging process. Some attempts at humor may veil anxieties about aging, disability, and death. Jokes about aging may reflect concerns about the loss of physical and mental abilities or may reveal fears of losing mental and physical abilities. Ageist jokes may reflect an individual's unsuccessful efforts at age concealment or may demean older people by ridiculing their sexuality or by criticizing their old-fashioned ways.

Ageist humor is frequently seen in birthday cards. Researchers Vasilikie Demos and Ann Jache found that a majority of cards they reviewed depicted aging in a negative light, especially in describing older women. The cards intended for female recipients centered on changes in appearance, particularly wrinkles and grey hair. Researchers Kathleen Dillon and Barbara Jones found that of those cards depicting an aging theme, most were negative and highlighted physical or mental loss or concealment. Psychologists Margaret Huyck and James Duchon examined the associations between coping styles regarding aging and relationships with those to whom one sends greeting cards. These researchers suggest that the humor displayed in birthday cards permits the sender to communicate otherwise hidden feelings. In this way, humor is used to deal with personal anxieties about aging.

Other mass media may reflect some of the ageist themes seen in greeting cards. The most influential form of mass media in America is television. Early research published in 1977 by Bruce Jeffreys-Fox found older characters to be rated less positively than younger ones. Gerontologist Robert Atchley analyzed 45 continuing television series that appeared on the three major networks during the 1979 season. He evaluated each series with regard to intergenerational themes and whether these themes included older people. He found that about 12% of the characters appeared to be 55 years old or older and 24 of the 45 series included intergenerational themes, with 8 of the 24 involving characters judged to be 55 or older. Atchley describes American television as "a medium responding to changing times." Communication specialist Jon Nussbaum and his associates report positive trends in both television programming and commercials. However, these same authors suggest that the portrayal of older adults in newspapers and popular magazines continues to be largely negative.

Attitudes toward older people are reinforced by both personal experience and the social myths that are communicated in society. The ageism that underlies stereotypes of older adults influences behavior, language, humor, and media images. While ageist stereotypes are still very much present in everyday life, there are signs of positive change.

DESCRIPTION OF ACTIVITIES

The Aging Stereotype Game

This activity examines the depth and prevalence of stereotypes as they relate to older adults. Numerous stereotypes, both positive and negative, influence perceptions of older people, and contribute to the ways in which older people are treated. In this exercise, learners are asked to identify positive and negative perceptions of older people.

Happy Birthday—Another Year!

This activity explores attitudes toward aging as reflected in birthday cards. Greeting cards provide a contemporary look at societal views of aging and older adults. In birthday cards, various themes are conveyed through written and visual images. Many of these themes refer to the aging process and allude to changes often associated with aging, such as alterations in appearance, memory, and sexual functioning. Learners are asked to analyze the messages that the cards communicate.

Older Adults and Television

In this activity, views of aging as reflected through the medium of television are examined. Because television represents such a pervasive influence, it often creates a long-lasting image of a particular segment of American society. In this exercise, learners are asked to watch television programs to gauge how elderly people are portrayed.

Myths About Aging

In this activity, learners interview three individuals regarding several popular myths about aging. Despite a great deal of scientific knowledge about older adulthood and aging, myths regarding chronological age, similarity, senility, serenity, productivity, and resistance to change persist. Learners are called upon to analyze possible reasons for the persistence of these myths.

The Aging Stereotype Game

PURPOSE

The purpose of this activity is to prompt the learner to think about common stereotypes about older adults. By working through this activity, the learner will be able to examine some of his or her own personal biases. Upon completion of this activity, the learner will be able to:

1. List common stereotypes associated with aging.

2. Discuss how ageism affects attitudes toward older adults.

TIME REQUIRED

45 minutes (25 minutes to complete the activity sheet and 20 minutes to discuss the activity in class)

PROCEDURE

1. The class is divided into groups of four to seven.

2. Each group develops lists of at least 15 negative and 15 positive beliefs concerning older people.

3. Each group chooses one person to record the stereotypes that are generated through group discussion.

4. After all groups have completed their lists, each group shares its lists with the entire class.

5. The instructor leads a class discussion that identifies themes emerging from the lists.

6. The instructor may lead a more general class discussion based on the following questions.

DISCUSSION QUESTIONS

1. Do you think that there is a relationship between one's attitudes toward older adults and one's knowledge of aging?

2. Cite three examples of ageism that you have observed.

3. Cite some examples of infantilization (viewing older adults as children). What effects can infantilization have on older people?

4. What are some of the similarities in the dynamics of ageism, racism, and sexism?

5. What can be done to reduce the level of ageism in our society?

The Aging Stereotype Game

In the spaces provided, list 15–20 negative stereotypes about older adults.

1. _____
2. _____
3. _____
4. _____
5. _____
6. _____
7. _____
8. _____
9. _____
10. _____
11. _____
12. _____
13. _____
14. _____
15. _____
16. _____
17. _____
18. _____
19. _____
20. _____

In the spaces provided, list 15–20 positive stereotypes about older adults.

1. _____
2. _____
3. _____
4. _____
5. _____
6. _____
7. _____
8. _____
9. _____
10. _____
11. _____
12. _____
13. _____
14. _____
15. _____
16. _____
17. _____
18. _____
19. _____
20. _____

```
┌─────────────────────────────────┐
│         │ Activity │            │
│         └──────────┘            │
│                                 │
│  Happy Birthday—Another Year!   │
│                                 │
└─────────────────────────────────┘
```

PURPOSE

The purpose of this activity is to uncover commonly held attitudes about age, as revealed through birthday cards. Upon completion of this activity, the learner will be able to:

1. Discuss several age-related themes found in greeting cards.

2. Describe both negative and positive stereotypic images of older adults and of aging as seen in birthday cards.

TIME REQUIRED

$1^1/_2$ hours (30 minutes to collect data on cards, 30 minutes to complete the activity sheets, and 30 minutes to discuss the activity in class)

PROCEDURE

1. Learners visit a greeting card store to study birthday cards, examining at least 10 greeting cards that depict older adults. An activity sheet is completed for each card analyzed.

2. Following completion of the activity sheets, the instructor divides the class into pairs. Learners discuss their responses to the activity sheet with their partners.

3. Following these discussions, the instructor leads a class discussion of the activity.

4. The instructor may lead a more general class discussion based on the following questions.

DISCUSSION QUESTIONS

1. What attitudes, positive or negative, are indicated in the themes of the birthday cards?

2. What are the various categories of themes seen in the birthday cards?

3. Give possible reasons to explain the jokes about the aging process and older adults that you may have found in the greeting cards you examined.

4. Does humor about aging reflect our fear of aging, fear of death, or both? Explain.

5. In what ways can humor have a positive effect on how we deal with aging?

6. Are there differences in birthday cards intended for men and those intended for women?

7. Did you find any birthday cards that presented a view of aging other than the typical "over-the-hill" one?

Happy Birthday—Another Year!

Analyze at least 10 birthday cards that describe a person getting older. Use one sheet of paper for each card.

Visual description of the card:

Words on the front cover:

Words on the inside:

Themes (e.g., losing memory or sexuality):

Positive or negative view of aging:

Comments:

```
┌─────────────────────────────┐
│         ┌──────────┐        │
│         │ Activity │        │
│         └──────────┘        │
│                             │
│   Older Adults and Television │
│                             │
└─────────────────────────────┘
```

PURPOSE

The purpose of this activity is to sensitize the learner to how television depicts older adults. Upon completion of this activity, the learner will be able to:

1. Analyze television programs regarding messages about aging.

TIME REQUIRED

$1^1/2$–$2^1/2$ hours (30–90 minutes to watch television, 30 minutes to complete the activity sheet, and 30 minutes to discuss the activity in class)

PROCEDURE

1. Learners watch at least one popular television program.
2. Learners complete an activity sheet for each program viewed.
3. The instructor leads a class discussion of the activity.
4. The instructor may lead a more general class discussion based on the following questions.

DISCUSSION QUESTIONS

1. Give examples of older characters that appear in television series. Are they depicted positively, negatively, or in a mixed fashion?
2. What were some of the intergenerational themes that you observed?
3. What were some of the intergenerational conflicts that you observed?
4. How are older adults depicted in commercials?

Older Adults and Television

Complete the activity sheet for each television show viewed.

Name of show:

Type of show (comedy or drama):

Ages of continuing characters:

Were there intergenerational themes (e.g., depiction of grandparent–grandchild or parent–child relationship)?

Did the theme involve older adults?

Were there conflicts between generations? If so, explain.

```
┌─────────────────────────────────┐
│        ┌──────────────┐          │
│        │   Activity   │          │
│        └──────────────┘          │
│                                  │
│      Myths About Aging           │
│                                  │
└─────────────────────────────────┘
```

PURPOSE

The purpose of this activity is to reveal various myths about aging. Upon completion of this activity, the learner will be able to:

1. Describe several popular myths about aging.

2. Describe the reactions to these myths of people from different age groups.

TIME REQUIRED

2½ hours (1 hour to conduct interviews, 1 hour to prepare interview summaries, and 30 minutes to discuss activity in class)

PROCEDURE

1. Using the activity sheet as a guide, learners conduct interviews with three people. One subject should be an adolescent, one should be middle aged, and one should be an older adult.

2. Learners prepare brief summaries of each interview, using the activity sheet.

3. The instructor leads a class discussion of the activity.

4. The instructor may lead a more general class discussion based on the following questions.

DISCUSSION QUESTIONS

1. Why do myths regarding aging persist?

2. In terms of personality, is there more variance in older people or in younger people? Why?

3. Why do you think that some older adults accept some of the myths associated with aging?

4. Discuss some specific strategies for changing public perceptions regarding common myths about aging.

Myths About Aging

Interview three people—one adolescent, one middle-age person, and one older adult—regarding myths about aging. Ask each person you interview to comment on the statements listed below. Prepare a one-page summary of each of the three interviews, and compare the responses of each.

1. Age is a good indicator of how old someone is.

2. Older people are more alike than are younger people.

3. For most people, old age is a wonderful time.

4. If people live long enough, they will probably become senile.

5. Younger people are more productive than older people.

6. Older workers are more likely than younger workers to resist change.

| Chapter 3 |

Physical Aging

THE CONCEPT OF AGE IS MULTIDIMENSIONAL. THE MOST COMMON CATEGORIZA-tions of age include chronological, biological, functional, psychological, and social age. People may be perceived as "old" or "young" depending on various conditions, such as physical health, mental attitude, and their role in society.

All of us are aging. From the moment we are born, the aging process begins. We may not even be aware of the changes that take place in our bodies. Each person ages at a different rate. One person may have grey hair at 20, while another person may not turn grey until 60. The process of aging affects each of us in different ways and at different times.

Changes that are generally associated with aging start during the third or fourth decade of one's life. Small changes, such as reduced ability to perform athletically, begin first. Dramatic changes, such as the changing of hair color or the wrinkling of skin, may occur later. It is important to re-member that if they live long enough, all people experience these changes. But they affect people differently.

Some changes occur because of the process of aging, while other changes are due to disease. It is important to know what changes are normal, and what changes need to be investigated so that proper treatment can be initiated.

Some common changes that occur with aging include: visual and hearing changes, changes in the skin, musculoskeletal changes, neurolog-ical changes, and changes in the gastrointestinal tract.

Visual changes often occur early in life, usually in one's 40s. Changes occur in the way the eye focuses and in its ability to accommodate to light. It may become more difficult to focus on reading material that is held close to the eye. An older person needs to hold material to be read at a distance in order to focus clearly. It may also become difficult to see at night, or to adjust to the glare of lights. Because of these changes, almost everyone will need some type of corrective lenses.

Hearing changes are more difficult to deal with, since it is less socially acceptable to wear a hearing aid than to wear glasses. Changes in auditory acuity are very gradual, beginning in one's 50s or 60s. Often a person accommodates to the hearing loss by increasing the volume of the television or asking people to repeat things. One of the effects of not being able to hear clearly is the feeling of isolation or paranoia. Therefore, it is important to treat the hearing change at an early stage so that the person can maintain a positive self-image and to continue to participate fully in life's events.

Musculoskeletal changes can be due to either normal aging or disease processes. As one ages, the spine shortens, causing a decrease in a person's height. Muscle mass also decreases if the body does not remain active and engage in exercise. Muscle strength also decreases 30%–50% between the ages of 20 and 60.

Arthritis is a common disease, affecting approximately 49% of people over age 65. This condition causes immobility and discomfort or pain that affect the daily living activities of many older people. Arthritis is a disease process, however, and not a part of the aging process. Many studies are currently being conducted to investigate causes and treatment of arthritis. Medication, exercise, and activity have been found to be important aspects of care in arthritis; much helpful information on dealing with arthritis is available from the Arthritis Foundation. Since arthritis can be disabling and interfere with activities of daily living, attention to the care and medical treatment of the disease over a long period is important.

In the absence of disease, older adults experience little change in the neurological system. There is a loss in the speed of learning, an increase in the amount of time required for the processing of information, and a decrease in reaction time. Memory loss and dementia are not normal changes that occur with aging, however. Two of the most common diseases that cause these symptoms are Alzheimer's disease and cerebrovascular disease.

Alzheimer's disease is a neurological disorder that results in the gradual, progressive loss of brain cells. The cause of Alzheimer's disease is not known and there is currently no treatment for the disease. The disease causes progressive memory loss, which eventually causes the person with the disease to forget how to perform even the simplest of tasks, such as eating and bathing.

Two physical changes—neurofibrillary tangles and senile plaques— are associated with Alzheimer's disease. Neurofibrillary tangles are bundles of ordinary brain filaments that have become twisted. Senile plaques are nerve cells that become surrounded by a protein. Both of these conditions are routinely seen in the brains of most older adults. However, in people with Alzheimer's disease, these conditions appear in particular parts of the brain in concentrations that are much greater than those seen in older adults without Alzheimer's disease.

Some 4 million Americans suffer from Alzheimer's disease and the anticipated increase in these numbers represents a major challenge to the health care system. More women than men have Alzheimer's disease, probably because of the greater longevity of women.

Management and care of the person with Alzheimer's disease generally falls to the family. Family members must cope not only with the loss of their loved one, but also with the burden of caring for a person 24 hours a day. The "36-hour day," a phrase coined by Nancy Mace and Peter Rabins in their book, *The 36-Hour Day*, suggests the intensity of care required by the person with Alzheimer's disease. In order to help families of people with Alzheimer's disease, the Alzheimer's Association, a national organization with local chapters throughout the country, provides educational materials and sponsors support groups for families.

Nutritional needs remain fairly constant throughout the lifespan. However, with age, one requires fewer calories. The challenge is to supply the body with needed nutrients (vitamins, minerals, carbohydrates) while reducing caloric intake. Many chronic diseases mandate that people change their diets. For instance, people who have diabetes must limit the intake of sugars; people with cardiac diseases must cut down on foods high in fat and cholesterol. These changes can be difficult.

Many of these normal changes (changes in vision, decreased muscle strength, and slowed reaction time) can limit one's ability to negotiate the environment effectively. Physical access may be easy when one is young, but even crossing a street can present a challenge to an older person. When a chronic illness requires that one use special equipment (e.g., a wheelchair, cane, walker, oxygen tank) to get around, a task as simple as getting to the doctor's office may be problematic. Although federal and state laws have been enacted that mandate the construction of buildings and environments that assist the independence of people with disabilities—most notably, the Americans with Disabilities Act—many areas exist that cannot be easily maneuvered by people with chronic illnesses.

Physical aging is inevitable. Disease and illness are not synonymous with aging, however. Healthy lifestyle patterns, which can begin at any age, can assist one in being healthy in old age or in minimizing the limitations imposed by chronic disease.

DESCRIPTION OF ACTIVITIES

Knowledge of Physical Aging Quiz

In this 15-item quiz, information regarding the physiology of aging is examined. Questionnaire items address such topics as pulse rate, osteoporosis, reaction time, skin elasticity, age spots, theories of physical aging, sensitivity to glare, hearing, chronic illness, life expectancy, sensitivity to taste, colorectal cancer, and arthritis.

Dietary Changes: A Meal Planning Strategy

Through this activity, learners plan several meals for an older adult who is advised to reduce both his weight and his cholesterol. By planning specific meals and determining the cost of those meals, learners come to appreciate the problems of adjusting to dietary limitations. A possible outgrowth of this activity could be an increased awareness of the importance of positive lifelong nutritional practices.

Ease or Dis-ease: Physical Access to Health Care

In this activity, physical barriers that interfere with an individual's ability to obtain health care services are examined. Through this exercise, learners explore environmental elements that may impede older people with disabilities in their use of health-related facilities. To determine if barriers exist, learners evaluate the accessibility of a hospital, a pharmacy, and a physician's office.

When Physical Function Is Limited

In this activity, a hypothetical situation is presented involving a visit to a physician and diagnosis of a chronic illness. Learners examine the concerns that may result following such an encounter. Instructors should be sensitive to the possibility that some learners may have experienced a similar situation in their own lives.

Knowledge of Alzheimer's Disease Quiz

In this activity, various aspects of Alzheimer's disease are examined. A 15-item questionnaire addresses the nature of Alzheimer's disease, changes that occur as a result of the disease, and support for caregivers.

Activity

Knowledge of Physical Aging Quiz

PURPOSE

The purpose of this activity is to allow the learner to examine his or her knowledge of the physiology of aging. Through this questionnaire, the learner will obtain information about physical aging. Upon completion of this activity, the learner will be able to:

1. Assess his or her knowledge of physical aging.

2. Increase his or her understanding of aging.

TIME REQUIRED

25 minutes (10 minutes to complete the quiz and 15 minutes to discuss the answers in class)

PROCEDURE

1. Learners take the quiz presented in the activity sheet.

2. The instructor reviews the answers to the quiz in class.

3. The instructor may lead a more general class discussion based on the following questions.

DISCUSSION QUESTIONS

1. What physical changes do you most associate with aging?

2. What is the relationship between aging and physical attractiveness?

3. What are some of the effects of diet and exercise on physical aging?

4. How does genetics affect physiological aging?

Knowledge of Physical Aging Quiz

Indicate whether each of the following statements is true or false.

		True	False
1.	With age, there is an increased ability of the pulse rate to return to normal following exercise.	_____	_____
2.	As people age, there is a tendency to lose calcium from bones.	_____	_____
3.	After age 70, 20% of the nerve cells of the cortex are lost each year.	_____	_____
4.	Reaction time stays the same throughout the lifespan.	_____	_____
5.	With age, there is loss of skin elasticity.	_____	_____
6.	Age spots develop because the cells lose their ability to produce pigment.	_____	_____
7.	Some theories of physical aging suggest that cells become damaged with age, causing them to function less efficiently.	_____	_____
8.	Middle-age and older persons are increasingly sensitive to glare.	_____	_____
9.	Older adults have more difficulty processing speech sounds than do middle-age persons.	_____	_____
10.	Almost half of all adults 65 and older have one or more chronic diseases.	_____	_____
11.	In the United States, life expectancy differs among various ethnic groups.	_____	_____

	True	False
12. With age, one's ability to taste becomes more sensitive.	_____	_____
13. The rate of colorectal cancer for people 75–79 is four times greater than that for people 55–59.	_____	_____
14. The most common health problem among older adults is arthritis.	_____	_____
15. With age, the walls of the arteries become less elastic.	_____	_____

```
┌─────────────────────┐
│      Activity       │
└─────────────────────┘
```

Dietary Changes:
A Meal Planning Strategy

PURPOSE

The purpose of this activity is to reveal the importance of proper nutrition for older adults and to teach the learner how to plan meals to reduce both weight and cholesterol level. Upon completion of this activity, the learner will be able to:

1. Discuss the importance of nutritional planning, both for those with special needs and the general public.

2. Plan meals based upon the need to reduce both caloric and cholesterol intake.

3. Appreciate the difficulty of adjusting to dietary changes.

TIME REQUIRED

4 hours (1½ hours to plan menus, 1 hour to check prices and nutritional content, 1 hour to complete the activity sheets, and 30 minutes to discuss the activity in class)

PROCEDURE

1. Using a nutrition book, learners plan meals for 3 days for the individual described in the activity sheet. Learners should use a book that contains charts containing breakdowns for cholesterol, fat, and calories. Two very good sources are: *Nutrition and Diet Therapy*, by S.B. Williams (Times Mirror-Mosby College Publishing, 1989) and *Sunset Low-Fat Cookbook* (Sunset Publishing, 1992).

2. Learners visit a grocery store and determine the cost of the meals they plan.

3. Learners complete the activity sheets.

4. Learners present their menu plans in class.

5. The instructor leads a class discussion of the activity.

6. The instructor may lead a more general class discussion based on the following questions.

DISCUSSION QUESTIONS

1. Why is food consumption considered an important source of ritual and security?

2. Why does food occupy a special place in the lives of many older adults?

3. What societal factors may contribute to poor dietary habits?

4. Why is it important to develop appropriate dietary patterns early in life?

Dietary Changes:
A Meal Planning Strategy

Read the case study and answer the questions that follow it.

Marvin Stone loves to eat. In fact, he structures his life around his three daily meals and various snacks. Since his wife, Trudy, died 3 years ago, food has taken center stage in Marvin's life; he eats anything and everything. Yesterday his physician, Dr. Pate, informed Marvin that his cholesterol level is high. Dr. Pate strongly encouraged Marvin to make an appointment with a dietician for nutritional counseling. The physician recommended that Marvin dramatically decrease the level of fat in his diet and lose some weight.

Various types of heart disease are linked with a high level of cholesterol, a harmful substance found in animal fats. Therefore, Marvin is advised by the dietician to eliminate or dramatically reduce his intake of foods high in saturated fats, foods such as eggs, whole milk, butter, and red meat. The dietician suggests that Marvin increase his intake of fruits, vegetables, fish, and poultry, and reduce his intake of sweets. This will be difficult, for there is nothing Marvin loves more than steak, ribs, pie, and ice cream.

The dietician provides Marvin with information about foods that will help him maintain a low-fat, low-calorie diet. He tells Marvin that his fat intake should be 30% or less of the total calories eaten per day. Since there are 9 calories in 1 gram of fat, Marvin can determine the percentage of fat intake by multiplying the total grams of fat in a product by 9, and dividing the result by the total number of calories in that food. For example, by reading the nutritional label on a can of vegetable soup, Marvin can determine that the soup contains 140 calories per serving as well as 3 grams of fat per serving. In order to calculate the number of calories of fat per serving, he multiplies 3 times 9 for a total of 27 grams; in order to determine the percentage of fat per serving, Marvin divides 27 by 140, which equals just over 19%.

Cholesterol intake should be limited to 300 milligrams or less per day. Milligrams of cholesterol are usually indicated on food packages.

Weight loss can be achieved by increasing the amount of exercise or by reducing the number of calories consumed each day. The total number of calories that need to be consumed per day depends on a person's size and level of activity. An average person consumes about 2,000–2,500 calories per day. Weight loss can be achieved by reducing the number of calories by 800–1,000 calories per day. This reduction of caloric intake will result in a slow, but steady loss of weight. A regular program of exercise, in conjunction with sensible eating, is the most effective method of reducing weight, and maintaining long-term weight control.

Although this new diet will require many changes, Marvin is ready to get started. After all, he would like to live for many more years. Marvin is scheduled to have his blood retested and to be weighed at the doctor's office in 3 months. He has never been one to back away from such a challenge.

1. Take on the role of Marvin. Plan meals for 3 days using the diet planning activity sheets. Make sure that the meals reflect the need to reduce your cholesterol level dramatically and to lose weight.

2. Using a nutrition book and food product labeling, determine the milligrams of cholesterol, the grams of fat, and the calories for meals for 3 days.

3. Visit a local grocery store and calculate the approximate cost of the meals and snacks.

4. Complete the activity sheets.

Meal Planning Strategy

Day 1

Meal/Item	Number of calories	Grams of fat	Milligrams of cholesterol	Cost
Breakfast				
Lunch				
Dinner				
Snack				
Total				

Meal Planning Strategy

Day 2

Meal/Item	Number of calories	Grams of fat	Milligrams of cholesterol	Cost
Breakfast				
Lunch				
Dinner				
Snack				
Total				

Meal Planning Strategy

Day 3

Meal/Item	Number of calories	Grams of fat	Milligrams of cholesterol	Cost
Breakfast				
Lunch				
Dinner				
Snack				
Total				

Meal Planning Summary

1. Calculate the total consumption of calories, fat, and cholesterol, and the total cost of meals for the 3 days of meal plans:

Day	Calories consumed	Grams of fat consumed	Milligrams of cholesterol consumed	Cost
1				
2				
3				
Total				

2. Did the meal plans meet the guidelines established by the dietician?

3. Which meals contributed the most calories, fat, and cholesterol?

4. Which specific items contributed the most calories, fat, and cholesterol?

5. What changes could you make to these meal plans to reduce the level of calories, fat, and cholesterol even further?

6. Which items contributed most to the cost of these meals?

7. What changes could be made to reduce the cost of these meals?

Ease or Dis-ease:
Physical Access to Health Care

PURPOSE

The purpose of this activity is to give the learner a sense of the obstacles encountered by frail older adults or older people with disabilities as they use health care services. Upon completion of this activity, the learner will be able to:

1. Describe several physical characteristics of hospitals, pharmacies, and physicians' offices.

2. Understand the difficulties encountered by frail older adults or older adults with disabilities in their attempt to avail themselves of medical services.

TIME REQUIRED

$2^1/_2$–$3^1/_2$ hours (2–3 hours to complete the activity sheets and 30 minutes to discuss the activity in class)

PROCEDURE

1. The class is divided into three groups. Learners in Group A evaluate three hospitals; learners in Group B evaluate three pharmacies; and learners in Group C evaluate physicians' offices in three different medical buildings. Visits can be made individually or in groups.

2. Following the site visits, learners complete the activity sheets.

3. The instructor leads a class discussion of the activity.

4. The instructor may lead a more general class discussion based on the following questions.

DISCUSSION QUESTIONS

1. What effect might the weather have on access to a health care facility for an older adult with a disability?

2. What are some general societal attitudes toward people with disabilities?

3. What kind of public transportation exists in your community? Is it accessible to people with disabilities?

4. What are your attitudes toward older people with disabilities?

5. Are there ways of increasing the independence of older adults with disabilities? What are they?

Ease or Dis-ease:
Physical Access to Health Care

Read the activity sheet before visiting the assigned sites. Complete one activity sheet for each facility visited.

1. Type of site:
   Hospital   Pharmacy   Physician's office

2. Are parking spaces provided for persons with disabilities?

   Yes ___   No ___

3. How many such parking spaces are available?

4. How close are the spaces to the entrance to the building?

5. Are there ramps or is there curbing from the parking spaces to the building?

6. Are there traffic controls, such as stop lights and crossing guards, to ensure safety in getting to the facility from the parking area? Is there a need for such controls?

7. Is the front door easy to open?

8. Is the door wide enough to accommodate a wheelchair?

9. Is the floor covered with carpet, tile, brick, or linoleum?

10. How far is the appropriate section of the building from the front door?

11. Is there sufficient seating in the waiting area?

12. Are there staff available to assist people with disabilities?

When Physical Function Is Limited

PURPOSE

The purpose of this activity is to make the learner aware of the psychological and physical effects of chronic illness on older adults. Upon completion of this activity, the learner will be able to:

1. Identify a chronic illness that may cause changes in a person's lifestyle.

2. Discuss the impact of a chronic illness on the daily life of an individual.

3. Evaluate personal feelings about living with a chronic illness.

TIME REQUIRED

2^1/$_2$ hours (2 hours to complete the activity sheet and 30 minutes to discuss the activity in class)

PROCEDURE

1. Learners complete the activity sheet individually.

2. Following completion of the activity sheets, the instructor leads a class discussion of the activity.

3. The instructor may lead a more general class discussion based on the following questions.

DISCUSSION QUESTIONS

1. Which conditions do you think have the greatest impact on daily functioning?

2. How can others assist the individual in an effort toward a return to adaptive living?

3. What are some of the different methods used by individuals to cope with chronic illness?

When Physical Function Is Limited

Older people often have to come to terms with living with a chronic disease, disability, and/or loss of function. Imagine that you have just come from your doctor's office. Your doctor has informed you that you have an incurable, chronic condition. (Examples of chronic conditions include arthritis, high blood pressure, high cholesterol, diabetes, chronic obstructive pulmonary disease [COPD], multiple sclerosis, muscular dystrophy, Parkinson's disease, and hearing impairment.) This chronic condition will require some adaptation and modification of your lifestyle. With adjustments, however, you will be able to live a normal life within limitations.

The doctor talked very quickly and you heard very little. You are overwhelmed by the thought of not being completely healthy. As you drive home, you begin to cry. "How can I find out more about this condition?" "Who can I talk to?" "What will my family think?" "How will they accept me?" "Will I be able to keep my job?" "How will my social life change?" "Will I tire easily?" "What is going to happen to my body?" "Will I be useless or a burden to others?"

Imagine that you are an older adult with a chronic condition. Choose a chronic condition of interest to you. The chronic condition you choose can be one of the examples cited here or you may choose another condition, such as one known to you through your own family history. Using library sources, research this condition and write a two-page essay that addresses these concerns. Use the following outline as a guide.

1. Identify the illness or condition.

2. Define the illness or condition.

3. What are the symptoms associated with the illness or condition?

4. How will the symptoms change your life?

5. Will you need any special equipment in order to function?

6. What organizations/associations may be able to provide you with information or support?

7. How much help will you need from family or friends to cook, clean, go shopping, pay bills, and so forth?

8. Do you think that family and friends will treat you differently? In what way?

9. If this actually happened to you, do you believe that you would develop a different outlook regarding living life each day?

```
┌─────────────────────────────────────────┐
│          ┌──────────────────┐           │
│          │     Activity     │           │
│          └──────────────────┘           │
│                                          │
│           Knowledge of                   │
│        Alzheimer's Disease Quiz          │
│                                          │
└─────────────────────────────────────────┘
```

PURPOSE

The purpose of this activity is to inform the learner about various aspects of Alzheimer's disease. Upon completion of this activity, the learner will be able to:

1. Answer basic questions about Alzheimer's disease.

TIME REQUIRED

30 minutes (15 minutes to complete the quiz and 15 minutes to discuss the answers in class)

PROCEDURE

1. Learners take the quiz presented in the activity sheet.

2. The instructor reviews the answers to the quiz in class.

3. The instructor may lead a more general class discussion based on the following questions.

DISCUSSION QUESTIONS

1. What are some of the problems affecting people with Alzheimer's disease and their families?

2. What are some of the approaches that professionals can use to assist family caregivers?

3. How can nursing home staff structure the day of the resident with Alzheimer's disease?

Knowledge of
Alzheimer's Disease Quiz

Indicate whether each of the following statements is true or false.

		True	False
1.	In the early stages of Alzheimer's disease, people tend to forget recent events.	_____	_____
2.	Personality changes, along with poor impulse control and impaired judgment, may present early in the course of Alzheimer's disease.	_____	_____
3.	Medication is helpful in treating Alzheimer's disease.	_____	_____
4.	Alzheimer's disease is an infectious process, which results in the loss of brain cells.	_____	_____
5.	The cause of Alzheimer's disease is not known.	_____	_____
6.	The diagnosis of Alzheimer's disease is based on clinical observation and presenting evidence.	_____	_____
7.	Caregivers and family members of people with Alzheimer's disease often experience depression.	_____	_____
8.	The progress of Alzheimer's disease is rapid, quickly leading to death.	_____	_____
9.	Alzheimer's disease is seen more frequently in men than in women.	_____	_____

		True	False
10.	A person could have both depression and Alzheimer's disease at the same time.	_____	_____
11.	The course of Alzheimer's disease is predictable.	_____	_____
12.	Helping patients with Alzheimer's disease learn new ways of coping improves their thinking and behavior.	_____	_____
13.	There is no cure for Alzheimer's disease.	_____	_____
14.	Support groups are helpful to caregivers of people with Alzheimer's disease.	_____	_____
15.	Neurofibrillary tangles and senile plaques are found in persons with Alzheimer's disease.	_____	_____

Chapter 4

Psychological Aging

AGING MAY BRING CHANGES IN SOME ATTITUDES, BEHAVIORS, AND ROLES. According to psychologist Paul Baltes and his associates, there are three types of influences on such changes: age-normative, history-normative, and nonnormative. A grade-school education is age-normative, since most people go through grade school at about the same age. History-normative influences, such as the Great Depression and the Vietnam War, have the potential of affecting many people during a given time frame. Typically, significant historical events have more of an impact upon some age groups than upon others. For example, adolescents and young adults were most directly affected by the Vietnam War. Nonnormative influences are tied to an individual's own life experiences. Included in this category are events such as the death of one's child. An individual's path of development occurs as a result of the interaction of age-normative, history-normative, and nonnormative life events. The specific effects of each of these few influences varies from one person to another.

There appears to be a great deal of stability in personality across adulthood. Psychologist Paul Costa and his colleagues looked at three traits in a large number of subjects: neuroticism (maladjustment), extroversion (warmth and assertion), and openness to experience (willingness to attempt new things). They found that most of their subjects showed much stability regarding these three traits and concluded that aging does not cause an individual's personality to change significantly. In attempting to explain the basic stability of adult personality, gerontologist Robert Atchley contends that adults try to maintain continuity in their thinking and behavior patterns. Atchley concedes that there is some change, but he argues that such change is adapted to by aging people through the continuity of their personalities.

Does an individual's concept of self change with age? Apparently, self-esteem often changes and changes for the better. If self-esteem is seen as the difference between a person's self-concept and ideal view of self,

then self-esteem can rise if there is an increase in the self-concept or a decrease in the ideal self. With age, an individual may come to terms with
the reality of not having achieved the youthful dream of becoming a fa-
mous artist, and with that realization may come a change in the perception of what one "should" be. Self-concept appears to increase with self-
acceptance, and for many persons, that occurs with age.

Self-concept is related to an adult's sense of independence. Independence involves physical, mental, financial, and social aspects. An ability
to manage one's physical needs and a degree of mobility are reflected by
physical independence. An individual demonstrates mental independence by being able to display problem-solving abilities. If a person has
the necessary economic resources to provide for food, shelter, medical
care, and so forth, he or she is said to be financially self-sufficient. Social
independence is the ability and capacity to rely on oneself. American culture encourages independence for all adults and relegates a diminished
status to those who are viewed as dependent. Many older people worry
that they will lose their independence and their value in society through
reliance on a fixed income or through a loss of ability to maintain their
own home.

If an individual's sense of independence can change with age, does a
person's overall mental health also change as a function of age? Re-
searcher Carolyn Aldwin and associates did find a relationship between
symptoms of psychological disorder and age. However, these same researchers found that there were great differences among the older people
they studied in terms of the degree to which they viewed themselves as
psychologically distressed. Apparently, for some older people, psychological problems increase with age, while for others, the perceived level of
psychological distress appears to decrease. It may be that certain changes
that accompany old age, such as the death of a spouse or a close friend,
contribute to emotional distress, while other changes, such as retirement
from a stressful or unsatisfying job, contribute to a perceived increase in
mental health.

One psychological disorder—depression—is common among older
adults. Data from the Duke Longitudinal Studies (as cited in Belsky, 1990)
appear to show that the precipitating factors for depression in women
may be different from those in men. Financial loss was seen as the most
likely precipitator for women, while men were more affected by a sudden
failure in health. There is increasing evidence that biological factors may
contribute to depression. Genetic predisposition and the malformation of
certain neurotransmitters may well play a significant role in the development of depressive disorders.

Another disorder affecting a small but growing number of older
adults is alcoholism. Although overall the rate of alcoholism drops dramatically with age, older people who begin drinking late in life appear to
have a much greater tendency than younger people to develop problems

with heavy drinking. The magnitude of some of the physical and psychological problems associated with heavy drinking may be due to the aging body's declining ability to tolerate alcohol. This phenomenon, known as late onset alcoholism, is not yet fully understood.

Some changes associated with aging appear to be experienced by almost all elderly people, while other changes are specifically related to some individuals or to a given time in history. Even though there are some inevitable changes that accompany aging, most older adults appear to adapt effectively. Most adults have personalities that remain largely stable throughout adulthood. However, for some older people, loss of independence, physical changes, and other distressors become more and more difficult to accommodate. For older adults whose adaptive abilities fail to function effectively, a variety of psychological difficulties may appear or existing conditions may worsen.

DESCRIPTION OF ACTIVITIES

The Timeline Interview

In this activity, the learner interviews an older adult, focusing on the interactions between the individual's life and important historical events. Using a list of questions as a framework, the learner explores how historical events affect the way a person perceives life. Areas covered include the individual's year of birth, childhood and adolescent recollections, work and family life, perceptions of the personal impact of some specific historical events, perceptions of current events, and plans for the future. It is important that learners interview someone previously unknown to them to ensure objectivity.

Maintaining Independence

In this activity, learners examine various aspects of independence in later adulthood. Participants are asked various questions about physical, mental, social, and economic independence and dependence. It is hoped that learners will gain an increased awareness of the need for independence of older persons, as well as their own need for continuing independence.

Fear of Falling

In this activity, learners are presented with the case of an older adult who has fallen and fears falling again. Because of the physical changes associated with the aging process, adaptations to the physical environment may be necessary. Learners are asked to analyze some of the psychological, physical, architectural, and social factors that affect this common fear. This activity allows the learner to evaluate some of the modifications that can be made to assist the older adult in maintaining independence and continuity.

Alcoholism in Later Life

In this activity, learners are presented with the case of a widow who has a problem with drinking. Learners assume the role of the woman's son and make a decision regarding possible intervention. Through this activity, learners will explore the psychological and social factors associated with alcoholism in later life.

┌─────────────────┐
│   Activity   │
└─────────────────┘

The Timeline Interview

PURPOSE

The purpose of this activity is to help the learner understand the relation-ship between an individual's life and significant historical events. Upon completion of this activity, the learner will be able to:

1. Use an individual lifeline and an historical timeline to understand an individual's life.

2. Assess the impact of historical change on the life of the individual.

TIME REQUIRED

2 hours (1¹/₂ hours to interview an older adult and 30 minutes to discuss the interviews in class)

PROCEDURE

1. Learners interview an older person. The person interviewed should not be a relative or close friend. The outline on the activity sheet should be used as a guide for conducting the interview, but questions should not be asked directly from the sheet. Learners should not take the guide with them when they conduct their interviews.

2. Learners write summaries of the interviews.

3. Learners discuss their summaries in class.

4. The instructor leads a class discussion of the activity.

5. The instructor may lead a more general class discussion based on the following questions.

DISCUSSION QUESTIONS

1. Describe an historical event that has had a significant impact on your life.

2. Have there been any chance encounters that have affected your life? Explain.

3. Did the older person you interviewed appear to enjoy speaking about the past?

4. Did the older person focus more on work or on family issues?

5. What historical event had the most impact on the older person interviewed?

6. What current events were of most interest to the older person interviewed?

The Timeline Interview

Use the following questions as the basis for an interview with an older adult.

1. When were you born?

2. Tell me about your childhood (hometown, parents, siblings, etc.).

3. Tell me about your teenage years (school, interests, friendships, etc.).

4. Tell me about your work and family life (jobs, spouse, children, etc.).

5. How did each of the following events influence you?
   a. Great Depression
   b. World War II
   c. Atom bomb
   d. Korean War
   e. Space program (Sputnik, landing on the moon)
   f. Civil rights movement
   g. Vietnam War
   h. Watergate
   i. Computers
   j. The Persian Gulf War
   k. Current events of today

6. Which of the following affects you most these days: family, social issues, or world events?

7. Tell me about your dreams and plans.

Maintaining Independence

PURPOSE

The purpose of this activity is to allow the learner to explore the concept of independence for older adults. Upon completion of this activity, the learner will be able to:

1. Define the concept of independence.

2. List the dimensions of independence.

3. Understand some of the resources necessary for older adults to maintain independence.

TIME REQUIRED

$1^1/_4$ hours (45 minutes to complete the activity sheet and 30 minutes to discuss the activity in class)

PROCEDURE

1. Learners complete the activity sheet individually.

2. The instructor leads a class discussion of the activity.

3. The instructor may lead a more general class discussion based on the following questions.

DISCUSSION QUESTIONS

1. Under what circumstances do we as a society encourage dependent behavior on the part of adults?

2. What aspect of your independence would you most like to keep? Why?

3. What services are available in your community that assist older people in maintaining their independence?

4. When should individuals start planning for financial independence in their older years?

Maintaining Independence

Prepare written answers to the following questions:

1. Why do we attach so much importance to the notion that adults should be independent?

2. What terms are commonly used to describe adults who are viewed as dependent?

3. What does it mean for an older adult to be independent? Be specific.

4. When is an older person no longer physically independent?

5. Give several examples of mental self-reliance.

6. How does access to transportation affect the level of independence of older people?

7. Describe the resources of an older adult whom you consider to be financially independent.

8. Many Americans believe that residing in one's own home is an important part of independence. Give specific reasons why many older people view the prospect of moving from their homes as a loss of independence.

9. Older people may view a move to a nursing home as the final blow to their independence. How can nursing home staff assist residents in their efforts to maintain independence?

Fear of Falling

PURPOSE

The purpose of this activity is to prompt the learner to think about problems associated with older people's fear of falling. Upon completion of this activity, the learner will be able to:

1. Discuss issues surrounding the fear of falling.

2. Describe some of the feelings associated with residing in one's own home and some of the concerns associated with moving to another home.

3. Describe some physical modifications that can make a home safe for frail older people.

TIME REQUIRED

40 minutes (20 minutes to read and analyze the case in small groups and 20 minutes to discuss the case in class)

PROCEDURE

1. The class is divided into small groups.

2. Each group analyzes the case found in the activity sheet and answers the questions that appear at the end of the case.

3. After the groups have discussed the case, the instructor leads a discussion of each group's findings.

4. The instructor may lead a more general class discussion based on the following questions.

DISCUSSION QUESTIONS

1. What are some of the physical conditions associated with aging that may contribute to falling?

2. Why is falling such a frightening experience for many adults?

3. Why is it that falls may lead to more severe injuries for older people than for younger ones?

4. Analyze your own home in terms of the likelihood of falling. How could you make your home safer?

Fear of Falling

With your group, read and analyze the case study and answer the questions that follow it.

Martha fell last year and bruised her hip. She is very much afraid of falling again. Martha lives in the home that she and her late husband purchased many years ago. The house holds wonderful memories. The house is too big for her—at least her children keep saying so—but the mortgage is paid and she loves the old house, her neighbors, and the neighborhood.

Still, Martha is afraid of falling, so afraid that she restricts her movement within the house. Rarely does she go upstairs, even though her sewing room is located on the second floor. She does not go outside alone for fear of falling on the steps leading to the front- and backyards. Only one of her children lives nearby, and he is busy in his small business, where he works about 14 hours a day. Martha wants to stay in the house, but she fears falling. The prospect of moving saddens her, but the fears surrounding falling are consuming her.

1. Are Martha's fears realistic? If not, how can she be encouraged to confront them?

2. What are Martha's options for dealing with her fears of falling?

3. Suppose Martha decides to stay in her house. What environmental changes could be made to reduce her chance of falling?

4. How can Martha's self-limiting behavior contribute to a lowering of self-esteem, increased isolation, and perhaps depression?

Alcoholism in Later Life

PURPOSE

The purpose of this activity is to familiarize the learner with the problems of and treatment options available for older alcoholics. Upon completion of this activity, the learner will be able to:

1. Describe several psychological and social factors associated with alcoholism in later life.

2. Discuss several treatment options for alcoholism among older adults.

TIME REQUIRED

45 minutes (25 minutes to complete the activity sheet and 20 minutes to discuss the activity in class)

PROCEDURE

1. The class is divided into groups of three or four.

2. Each group reads the case study presented on the activity sheet and answers the case questions.

3. The instructor leads a class discussion of the activity.

4. The instructor may lead a more general class discussion based on the following questions.

DISCUSSION QUESTIONS

1. What are the differences between early-onset and late-onset alcoholism?

2. What problems are associated with prescription drug abuse among older people?

3. Are older alcoholics more difficult to detect than younger ones?

4. Why do some older people start drinking heavily?

Alcoholism in Later Life

Read and analyze the case study and answer the questions that follow it.

Margaret is a 70-year-old woman with many friends, including a 75-year-old man. Margaret and her friends get together three or four times a week to play cards or to go out to dinner. There is always alcohol available at these social gatherings. Over the past several months, Margaret has been drinking three or four cocktails each evening, even when she is not with her friends.

When her late husband was alive, Margaret drank sparingly. Her husband was a disciplined man, who frowned on all excesses, including drinking.

Margaret's son, Marvin, lives nearby. Marvin and his wife have been concerned about Margaret. At a family gathering the previous Sunday, Margaret had appeared to be drunk. The next day in a phone conversation with her son, Margaret mentioned that she is having trouble remembering some of the events of the day before.

1. What psychological factors may be contributing to Margaret's heavy drinking?

2. What social factors may be contributing to Margaret's heavy drinking?

3. If you were Marvin, what would you do about your mother's drinking?

4. How might Margaret resist her son's intervention?

5. In your community, what are the available treatment options for helping Margaret?

Chapter 5

Sexuality and Aging

SOCIETAL VIEWS OF SEXUALITY IN OLDER ADULTS ARE GREATLY INFLUENCED BY myths. These myths may include the following:

1. Sex and sexuality are more appropriate for younger people than for older people.

2. The sexual interests and behaviors of older people are funny or cute.

3. Older people are physically unattractive.

4. Older people who are sexually active are weird or deviant.

5. Older people are unable to have sexual intercourse.

These myths form the basis for many comments that poke fun at sexuality—or the supposed loss of sexuality—in older adults. Many stand-up comedians use such jokes, which are almost guaranteed to arouse a nervous chuckle from those members of the audience who misunderstand the lifelong nature of human sexuality.

Sexuality encompasses more than just physical activities. It refers to an individual's self-perceptions of being attractive as a sexual partner. The ways in which one dresses, converses with peers, and daydreams are all affected by sexuality and sexual identity. Whether an individual is sexually active or not, that person may still be sexual, as reflected in the ways he or she chooses to dress and interact.

People begin to understand their sexual identity very early in childhood. They mature sexually with puberty, but human sexuality continues throughout the life cycle, taking different forms depending on an individual's preferences and opportunities.

Some physical changes are often associated with aging and the sexual response. Sex researchers Masters and Johnson found that women generally experience more minor changes in the physiology of sex than do men. For women, specific changes are associated with age. In younger women, for example, breast size increases during arousal, something that usually does not happen in older women. With menopause comes a depletion of estrogen, which may cause the vaginal walls to thin, resulting in dryness. The walls of the vagina become smoother and thinner and the vagina shortens, with both the clitoris and labia decreasing in size. With age, vaginal secretions may decrease for women who do not remain sexually active.

Generally, men experience more major age-related changes in the physiology of sex than do women. Typically, it takes longer for older men to get an erection than younger men, but they may maintain the erection longer. The lessened need to ejaculate appears to be related to a reduction in the amount of seminal fluid. After the age of 50, the time interval necessary between erections lengthens. Older men may have to wait up to 12–24 hours after ejaculation before being able to have another erection. Also, the penis becomes flaccid sooner after ejaculation than it does in younger men. These changes may be misunderstood by older couples who fear impotence. Reassurance must be given to indicate the normal process of changes in older people.

Illness or disability may affect sexual expression. Sexual partners may avoid or limit sexual contact because of pain associated with sexual activities. More often, chronic illness affects feelings of self-worth and sexual adequacy, which may affect the sexual relationship of an elderly couple.

Many fears associated with the physical risk of sexual practices of older people have not been substantiated. For example, after consultation with a physician, many cardiac patients are eventually able to resume prior sexual practices. Some physical conditions do have a permanent impact on the physiology of sex, however. For example, prostatectomies often lead to impotence. In some cases, penile implants can be used to allow the man to maintain an erection. Diabetes may also cause impotence, and arthritis may result in a sufficient amount of weakness and pain to discourage sexual activities. Prescription drugs and alcohol may also affect both the desire for sex and the sexual response. Drugs used to treat hypertension, as well as sedatives, antidepressants, and antihistamines, may contribute to sexual dysfunction.

Psychologist Janet Belsky summarized several longitudinal studies and found that there was a gradual decline in sexual interest with age. About three-fourths of the subjects who were in their 60s reported that they continued to engage in sexual intercourse, and a larger percentage indicated the presence of sexual feelings. As respondents entered their 70s, however, many reported abstaining from intercourse, with about four-fifths giving up intercourse by their 80s or 90s. At every age, women mentioned significantly less sexual interest than did men, and by their late 60s, only one woman in five reported having an interest in sex. These differences between the responses of males and females may well be due to cultural prohibitions, which in the past have suggested to women that they are not supposed to be as interested in sex as are men.

One of the most significant factors influencing sexual behavior among older people is the large disparity between the number of men and women. Among people age 65 and over, there are almost one and a half times as many women as men. This limits the availability of older men as sexual partners.

The continuing sexuality of older people may be an uncomfortable reality for some adult children and long-term care staff members. Unknowingly, staff may demean older residents by teasing or ridiculing them when they express physical desire toward another resident. Some facilities attempt to control sexual behavior by minimizing residents' privacy. This infringes on the basic rights of the resident. Scholars Peter Lichtenberg and Deborah Strzepek suggest some useful guidelines in assessing resident competencies regarding intimate relationships. These include the resident's awareness of the relationship, the individual's ability to avoid exploitation, and the resident's awareness of potential risks.

People continue to be sexual throughout their lives. There are some changes that may accompany the sexual response as people age. Illness, disability, and medications may profoundly affect sexual interest and performance, but much of the impact appears to be psychological, based upon societal myths associated with sexuality in older adults.

DESCRIPTION OF ACTIVITIES

Knowledge of Sexuality and Aging Quiz

Many myths prevail regarding sexuality and aging. This activity provides information about sexuality and older adults. Information is conveyed in the form of a quiz that examines learners' knowledge and dispels misconceptions about sexuality in older people.

Sexuality and the Older Adult

In this activity, learners comment on issues surrounding sexuality and older adults. Learners describe sexual practices; perceptions of sexuality; and physiological, psychological, and social factors affecting sexuality. Learners also consider how age norms might affect the sexuality of older people.

The Empty Bed

Through use of a case study, this activity explores issues of sexuality and self-image. The case study describes a widow who is confronted with the loss of her husband and the reality of the empty space in the bed she and her spouse had shared. The learner is asked to identify some myths surrounding aging and sexuality; the need for touch; and the relationships among self-image, sexuality, and aging. Learners are also asked to think about how they would counsel the widow.

```
┌─────────────────────┐
│      Activity       │
└─────────────────────┘

        Knowledge of
   Sexuality and Aging Quiz
```

PURPOSE

The purpose of this activity is to increase the learner's knowledge of sexuality and aging. Upon completion of this activity, the learner will be able to:

1. Assess his or her knowledge of sexuality in older adults.

2. Explore attitudes regarding sexuality and aging.

TIME REQUIRED

30 minutes (15 minutes to complete the quiz and 15 minutes to discuss the answers in class)

PROCEDURE

1. Learners take the quiz presented in the activity sheet.

2. The instructor reviews the answers to the quiz in class.

3. The instructor may lead a more general class discussion based on the following questions.

DISCUSSION QUESTIONS

1. Why do some people have difficulty perceiving their parents and grandparents as sexual persons?

2. What are some of the changes in the physiology of sex that often accompany aging?

3. What impact do staff attitudes have on the sexual practices of older people living in long-term care facilities?

4. What purpose do jokes about sexuality and aging serve?

5. What are some common stereotypes about sexuality and older persons?

6. Do you believe that your own sexuality will be affected by aging? Explain.

Knowledge of Sexuality and Aging Quiz

Indicate whether each of the following statements is true or false.

	True	False
1. Older men are more sexually active than older women.	_____	_____
2. People who are more sexually active in middle age are more likely to be sexually active in old age than people who were less active.	_____	_____
3. The majority of older women are sexually unresponsive.	_____	_____
4. Diabetes can cause impotence in older men.	_____	_____
5. Sexual activities may serve a therapeutic function for many older adults.	_____	_____
6. Sexual activity tends to diminish in old age more because of social and psychological factors than biological and physical ones.	_____	_____
7. Older men may maintain their erections longer than younger men.	_____	_____
8. The amount of vaginal lubrication decreases with age.	_____	_____
9. Compared to younger adults, older adults need more time for sexual stimulation before intercourse.	_____	_____

	True	False
10. Prostate dysfunction can affect sexual responsiveness.	_____	_____
11. Because older people are fragile, sexual intercourse can be dangerous to their health.	_____	_____
12. A significant problem facing older women who wish to remain sexually active is the limited number of older men.	_____	_____
13. Masturbating may have physiological benefits for older people.	_____	_____
14. Lack of privacy is a major problem for people who live in long-term care facilities and wish to remain sexually active.	_____	_____
15. Some older men who are unable to get erections may benefit from penile implants.	_____	_____

Sexuality and the Older Adult

PURPOSE

The purpose of this activity is to provide the learner with an opportunity to examine his or her perceptions of sexuality and older adults. Upon completion of this activity, the learner will be able to:

1. Review factors that affect an older person's sexual behavior.

2. Develop an understanding of aging and sexuality.

TIME REQUIRED

1 hour (20 minutes to complete the activity sheet, 20 minutes to discuss the activity in small groups, and 20 minutes to discuss the activity as a class)

PROCEDURE

1. Learners complete the activity sheet individually.

2. Following completion of the activity sheets, the instructor divides the class into small groups to discuss the activity.

3. Following these discussions, the instructor leads a class discussion of the activity.

4. The instructor may lead a more general class discussion based on the following questions.

DISCUSSION QUESTIONS

1. What are some stereotypes regarding sex and older people?

2. What illnesses might affect sexual functioning?

3. Does the ratio of older women to older men affect sexual behavior?
    Explain.

4. What effects do prescription drugs have on sexual behavior?

5. Why are people who are more sexually active in middle age more
    likely to be sexually active as older adults?

6. What age norms influence our concepts of sexuality and aging?

7. Why do we tend to associate sexuality with adolescence and young
    adulthood?

Sexuality
and the Older Adult

Write a one- or two-paragraph answer to each of the following questions.

1. How do you think sex is practiced by people over 65 years old? How is it different from sex for younger people?

2. In terms of sexuality, do you think that people view themselves differently in their later years? Why or why not?

3. What physiological factors might affect the sexual behavior of older people?

4. What psychological factors might affect the sexual behavior of older people?

5. What social factors might affect sexual behavior among older people?

```
┌─────────────────────┐
│      Activity       │
└─────────────────────┘


      The Empty Bed
```

PURPOSE

The purpose of this activity is to stimulate the learner's thinking about the sexual implications of being alone. Following completion of this activity, the learner will be able to:

1. Identify common myths related to sex and aging.

2. Recognize the need for touch and affection throughout the lifespan.

TIME REQUIRED

45 minutes (20 minutes to complete the activity sheet and 25 minutes to discuss the activity in class)

PROCEDURE

1. Learners read the case in the activity sheet.

2. Learners choose partners with whom they feel comfortable talking about the case, and work with their partners to complete the activity sheet.

3. Learners discuss the case with their partners, using the questions following the case study.

4. The instructor leads a class discussion of the activity.

5. The instructor may lead a more general class discussion based on the following questions.

DISCUSSION QUESTIONS

1. What are some common myths that are associated with sex, sexuality, and aging?

2. What are your attitudes and feelings regarding sex, sexuality, and aging?

3. Do you believe that sex is inseparable from human relationships? Explain.

4. What physiological factors may affect human sexuality?

5. Do you think sexual expression is more difficult for an older person than a younger person?

The Empty Bed

With your partner, read and analyze the case study and answer the questions that follow it.

Clara awoke, turned to her side, touched the opposite side of the bed, and found it empty. A surge of unexpected feelings rushed through her body. The stark reality of being alone was almost overwhelming. Thoughts raced through her mind. "How could Harry leave me? Will I ever feel like a woman again? I want to be touched. I know I'm attractive. What can I do to feel loved?"

Clara pondered these thoughts for a few minutes. "I've heard it said, 'If you don't use it, you'll lose it.' Oh dear, oh dear! With the dreaded diseases today, who would even take a chance? Will I ever again find someone to love, to make me feel like a woman? When will I be myself again?"

1. What common sexual myths are evident in Clara's thoughts?

2. How does self-image relate to aging and sexuality?

3. Discuss ways Clara might find to be touched and loved.

4. If Clara confided her thoughts to you, what would you recommend to her?

Chapter 6

Family Issues in Aging

FAMILY ISSUES ARE CENTRAL TO AN UNDERSTANDING OF OLDER ADULTS. AS older adults retire and see their children leave home, they have more time to spend together, possibly changing the nature of their relationships. For many couples, the increase in the amount of time they can spend alone with each other is viewed as a reward for the years of hard work both inside and outside the home; most older people are comfortable with the change in their role associated with retirement and the "empty nest." According to gerontologist Robert Butler, about two thirds of older couples report that their marriage is satisfying. For couples whose marriages have been unhappy, however, the increase in time spent together may exacerbate the sources of conflict. Divorce among older couples—something that was rare a generation ago—is more and more common.

Most older couples eventually become grandparents, an experience that most older people cherish. Gerontologist Robert Atchley describes research showing that almost half the people studied reported having an active relationship with their grandchildren, about 30% reported having passive relationships, and 20% reported having distant relationships. Other scholars have noted that younger grandparents tend to be more active than older ones, and that women tend to assume the grandparent role more easily than men do.

Psychologist Lillian Troll has suggested that grandparents serve an important function as "family watchdogs," stepping in to help their children and grandchildren when needed. This role has become particularly important as the rate of divorce among couples with young children rises. Researchers Sarah Matthews and Jetse Sprey found that about half of the grandparents they studied maintained friendly relationships with their son's or daughter's former spouse following a divorce. This relationship was more likely to be maintained with ex-wives than with ex-husbands.

Relationships between family members also change as personal and societal expectations shift over time. Adolescents are expected to become

105

increasingly self-sufficient as they develop into adults; adults with aging parents are expected to take on some responsibility for caring for their parents. Sometimes adult children are required to care for a parent with a chronic illness. This role usually falls to the older adult's daughter or daughter-in-law. Gerontologist Elaine Brody has referred to women in this role as "women in the middle," sandwiched between the needs of their children, husbands, and dependent parents or parents-in-law.

One common myth is that American families typically abandon their older members. There is no evidence to support the notion that this practice is widespread. According to gerontologist Victor Cicirelli, many parents and children maintain a continuing pattern of mutual assistance. Parents may help their adult children by babysitting their grandchildren, while adult children may help their parents by driving them places or performing physically demanding household chores. Cicirelli reports that about 80% of older people have living children, and that most of them are in contact with them. Most adult children, moreover, feel "close" or "very close" to their parents.

Although most older adults have children, the number of older people without children is growing. Such people may draw upon siblings, friends, or professional caregivers for assistance as they age. As the number of older people without children grows, the demands on public resources will also increase.

Undoubtedly the greatest change affecting older couples is the death of a spouse. Since on average women live longer than men and tend to marry men older than themselves, women tend to outlive their spouses. Widowhood can seriously affect a person's sense of self, especially for men and women who were married for many years and who define themselves largely in terms of their marital roles. Widowhood can also bring loneliness, financial loss, and a lack of opportunity for sexual expression. Nevertheless, after a period of mourning and grief, most widows and widowers gradually adjust to their new roles.

Older adults should be viewed in the context of their families, since the quality of their family relationships greatly affects their overall satisfaction with life. Although conflicts with adult children may occur, most older adults enjoy satisfying relationships with their spouses, adult children, and grandchildren. Most older adults also enjoy the "empty nest," although couples whose marriages were conflictual earlier in life may find the extra time they spend together after retirement unendurable and may actually divorce.

DESCRIPTION OF ACTIVITIES

The Generation Gap Rap

In this activity, learners compare and contrast their attitudes and values with those of their parents, their adolescent children, and/or their adult children. Learners are asked to compare and contrast their views on politics, religion, civil rights, money, technology, violence, and sexuality. Those learners who have adolescent or adult children are encouraged to assess whether their beliefs are closer to those of their parents or their children.

Adult Children and Their Parents

In this activity, relationships between adult children and their parents are examined. Learners interview an adult acquaintance who has at least one living parent. Using a series of questions as a guide, learners explore patterns of affection, aid, and interaction between parent and child. Questions relate to the frequency, length, and quality of visits with parents; patterns of mutual assistance; expressions of affection; and relationships between siblings and parents.

The Roles of Grandparents: The Ideal Versus the Real

In this activity, learners contrast their idealization of the role of grandparents with their own experience. Learners analyze the grandparent–grandchild relationship from the viewpoint of both parties, describe an "ideal" grandparent, and project to the time when they may be grandparents. This learning experience may be especially useful in a class comprised of learners of a wide range of ages. Older learners may express views that are somewhat different from those of younger learners.

Loss and Widowhood

Widowhood can dramatically affect an individual's identity. Often, married people define themselves largely through their marital roles. In addition to changes in identity, widowhood can bring loneliness and a decrease in opportunities for companionship and sexual expression. In this activity, learners examine losses associated with widowhood, and describe possible coping strategies for dealing effectively with these losses.

Far From Home

In this activity, learners examine issues associated with geographical separation between older adults and their children. Competing demands and past conflicts may inhibit an individual's capacity to respond to the concurrent needs of aging parents, siblings, children, and spouse. Through this case, learners explore the possible role of guilt in responding to crises facing aging parents. Practical problem-solving strategies are analyzed through small group and class discussions.

```
┌─────────────────────────────────┐
│         ┌───────────┐           │
│         │  Activity │           │
│         └───────────┘           │
│                                 │
│                                 │
│    The Generation Gap Rap       │
│                                 │
│                                 │
└─────────────────────────────────┘
```

PURPOSE

The purpose of this activity is to provide a framework for comparing similarities and differences between one's own attitudes and lifestyles and those of one's parents and/or adolescent/adult children. Upon completion of this activity, the learner will be able to:

1. Express his or her views on issues of values and lifestyle.

2. Compare perceived views of parents and/or children on the same issues.

TIME REQUIRED

45 minutes (20 minutes to complete the activity sheet and 25 minutes to discuss the activity in class)

PROCEDURE

1. Learners complete the activity sheet individually.

2. Following completion of the activity sheets, the instructor divides the class into groups of three or four to discuss the activity sheet.

3. The instructor leads a class discussion of the activity.

4. The instructor may lead a more general class discussion based on the following questions.

DISCUSSION QUESTIONS

1. In what ways are your parents' or children's attitudes different from yours?

2. Why do you think your children or parents hold the political beliefs that they do?

3. How do your views on money differ from those of your parents or your children?

4. How do your views on technology differ from those of your parents and your children?

5. Is there a generation gap? Explain.

The Generation Gap Rap

Complete the following table. First describe your own views, then describe what you think your parents' views are. If you have adolescent or adult children, indicate what you believe their views are.

Issues	Your views	Your parents' views	Your adolescent or adult child's views
Political party			
Religious practices			
Civil rights			
Money			
Technology			
Violence			
Sex and sexuality			

Adult Children and Their Parents

PURPOSE

The purpose of this activity is to provide the learner with a framework for assessing the relationship between older parents and their adult children. Upon completion of this activity, the learner will be able to:

1. Analyze several dimensions of the relationships between parents and their adult children.

TIME REQUIRED

1$\frac{1}{2}$ hours (1 hour to complete the activity and 30 minutes to discuss the activity in class)

PROCEDURE

1. Learners conduct brief interviews with acquaintances who have either adult children or parents over 65.

2. After conducting the interview, learners complete the activity sheet.

3. The instructor leads a class discussion of the activity.

4. The instructor may lead a more general class discussion based on the following questions.

DISCUSSION QUESTIONS

1. How is the "greying of America" affecting family relationships?

2. How far do you live from your parents or grandparents? How often do you visit them?

3. What effects will the increasing rate of female employment have on the relationship between adult children and their parents?

4. Discuss the myth that adult children tend to abandon their parents.

5. What effects may the divorces of adult children have on their relationships with their parents?

6. How do adult children and their parents display affection?

Adult Children and Their Parents

Interview an adult acquaintance who has at least one living parent. Use the questions listed here as a guide, but do not read from this list during the interview. Upon completion of your interview, prepare a summary of the information obtained during your interview.

1. How old is the person interviewed?

2. How far does the person live from his or her parents?

3. How often does the person speak with his or her parents on the telephone?

4. How often does the person see his or her parents?

5. How long are the visits?

6. Does this person provide any assistance to his or her parents? How?

7. Do either of this person's parents help him or her with any service (e.g., child care)?

8. Do either of this person's parents provide any financial assistance?

9. Does the person provide any financial assistance to his or her parents?

10. How is affection expressed between the person interviewed and his or her parents?

11. Does the person have siblings?

12. Describe the relationships between these siblings and their parents.

The Roles of Grandparents: The Ideal Versus the Real

PURPOSE

The purpose of this activity is to compare the expectations and realities of grandparenthood. Upon completion of the activity, the learner will be able to:

1. Describe the relationship with his or her own grandparents.

2. Distinguish between the actual and the expected roles of grandparents.

3. Evaluate the grandchild–grandparent relationship from the point of view of both parties.

TIME REQUIRED

40 minutes (20 minutes to complete the activity sheet and 20 minutes to discuss the activity in class)

PROCEDURE

1. Learners complete the activity sheet individually.

2. Following completion of the activity sheets, the instructor divides the class into pairs. Learners discuss their responses to the activity sheet with their partners.

3. Following these discussions, the instructor leads a class discussion of the activity.

4. The instructor may lead a more general class discussion based on the following questions.

DISCUSSION QUESTIONS

1. Do some adult children overestimate the joys of grandparenting?

2. Why are grandparents sometimes considered the family watchdog?

3. Is the grandparent–grandchild relationship romanticized by our culture?

4. What are some of the problems that may develop between grandparents and their adult children over the rearing of the grandchildren?

The Roles of Grandparents: The Ideal Versus the Real

Prepare written responses to the following questions.

1. What recollections do you have of your grandparents? Be as specific as possible.

2. What are the benefits of being a grandparent?

3. What are some possible drawbacks of being a grandparent?

4. What are the benefits to a grandchild of having a relationship with a grandparent?

5. Describe an "ideal" grandparent.

6. One day you may be a grandparent. How do you believe that you may act in that role?

Loss and Widowhood

PURPOSE

The purpose of this activity is to help the learner understand the losses associated with widowhood among older adults. Upon completion of this activity, the learner will be able to:

1. Identify the losses associated with widowhood.

2. Discuss possible differences between the experience of widowhood for men and for women.

3. Examine possible coping strategies for dealing with loss.

TIME REQUIRED

45 minutes (25 minutes to complete the activity sheet and 20 minutes to discuss the activity in class)

PROCEDURE

1. The class is divided into groups of three to five.

2. Each group completes the activity sheet.

3. Each group chooses one person to record and present the group's findings to the entire class.

4. The instructor leads a class discussion on the activity.

5. The instructor may lead a more general class discussion based on the following questions.

DISCUSSION QUESTIONS

1. If you became a widow or widower after many years of marriage, what might be the greatest loss for you?

2. Do widows and widowers frequently remarry? Explain.

3. Are there differences between the adaptive patterns of widows and widowers? Explain.

4. What kinds of support can adult children offer recently widowed parents?

5. Discuss the notion of spouse sanctification.

6. How might one's identity be tied to being married?

Loss and Widowhood

For each of the following categories, give at least one example of a loss associated with widowhood.

1. Self-identity

2. Loneliness

3. Changes in family roles

4. Changes in the relationship between the widowed parent and his or her adult children

5. Changes in the relationship between the widowed person and his or her extended family

6. Other changes

Far From Home

PURPOSE
The purpose of this activity is to make the learner aware of the problem of separation between parents and their adult children. Upon completion of this activity, the learner will be able to:

1. Discuss some of the problems that may arise when adult children live far from their parents.

2. Discuss competing demands on adult children of parents with physical or emotional problems.

3. Describe some of the possible conflicts among siblings when dealing with the health needs of their parents.

TIME REQUIRED:
30 minutes (15 minutes to complete the activity sheet and 15 minutes to discuss the activity in class)

PROCEDURE
1. The class is divided into groups of three or four.

2. Each group completes the activity sheet.

3. Following completion of the activity sheets, each group presents its findings to the entire class.

4. The instructor leads a class discussion of the activity.

5. The instructor may lead a more general discussion based on the following questions.

DISCUSSION QUESTIONS

1. In what ways are middle-age people with children and living parents "sandwiched"?

2. What are some specific problems that may arise when adults live hundreds or thousands of miles from their parents?

3. What role might guilt play in the relationship between adults and their parents when family members are separated geographically?

4. What are some practical ways for adult siblings to maintain good relationships with one another?

Far From Home

Read and analyze the case study and answer the questions that follow it.

It has been difficult living so far from home all these years. Not that life hasn't been good for Juanita. After high school, she met her husband, José, who has been a wonderful mate and father to their four children. Juanita occasionally gets lonely, with José, a truck driver, gone much of the time.

Juanita lives 2,000 miles from where she was raised. Her sister, Carmela, and two brothers, Roberto and Sam, live within 20 miles of their parents' home. Juanita has made an effort to remain close to her parents through frequent telephone calls, letters, and yearly visits.

Last night, her older brother, Roberto, called to discuss his concerns regarding their father, whose health is failing. Last year the father suffered a mild stroke. He is tired, withdrawn, and sometimes appears to be confused. Their mother, always the organizer and caretaker of the family, seems very depressed, has stopped seeing her friends, and no longer participates in church activities.

Roberto wants Juanita's help. Wasn't she always Dad's favorite? Could she come and stay with their parents for a month or so? Juanita is truly torn by these demands. What about her job at the bakery? What about her children? What about José?

Juanita and Roberto have remained close, but Juanita has not been in frequent contact with Sam and Carmela. Roberto feels overwhelmed. His own marriage ended in divorce last year and he is involved in an ongoing conflict with his ex-wife over visitation with their three children. The size of the child support payments has forced him to take a second job.

Juanita loves her parents and wants to help them in any way that she can. It really is difficult being so far from home.

1. What are some of the concerns expressed by Juanita's brother, Roberto?

2. What are some of Juanita's concerns?

3. How might past family issues prevent the four adult children from co-operating in assisting their parents?

4. What about Juanita's parents? What is their role in defining and solving the problem?

5. What options could be considered?

Chapter 7

Maximizing Choices

HUMAN BEINGS APPEAR TO THRIVE WHEN THEY ARE IN A POSITION TO MAKE their own choices. Many people look forward to a time in life when responsibilities such as child rearing and a full-time job are no longer pressing concerns, and they will have more opportunities to engage in activities providing more personal satisfaction. This chapter examines several issues related to personal choice: work, retirement, finances, volunteerism, and political concerns of older adults.

Until the early part of this century, older Americans typically remained in their jobs until they died; retirement was not common. Until pensions became common, people tended to work as long as they could physically do so. With the development of labor unions and collective bargaining, more and more older workers gained pension benefits, thus allowing them to retire from their jobs.

Robert Atchley, an authority on retirement, suggests that there are three distinct reasons older people retire:

1. They are interested in pursuing other activities.

2. They find it difficult to continue working because of failing health.

3. They are unable to find work.

Because of legal changes striking down most instances of mandatory retirement age, many people continue to work full- or part-time. Nevertheless, stereotypes about elderly workers persist. Gerontologist Georgia Barrow lists the following stereotypes:

1. Older workers are not as productive as younger ones.

2. Older workers do not have the necessary physical endurance to work full-time.

3. Older workers are rigid and resist change.

4. Older workers do not interact well with younger employees or with the general public.

5. Older workers learn slowly.

6. Older workers lack ambition and creativity.

The evidence does not support these generalities. Nevertheless, such stereotypes contribute to ageist attitudes and discriminatory behaviors and policies in the workplace. Barrow contends that older workers tend to be at least as competent as younger workers. According to her, older workers have superior attendance records, are more likely to be stable and happy, and produce as much as younger workers.

Most people look forward to retirement, although attitudes toward retirement seem to be closely linked to finances. People who expect to be comfortable financially tend to look forward to retirement. People who are dissatisfied with their work lives may also look forward to retirement, although their lack of financial resources may create some dread concerning a decline in income following the loss of a paycheck.

The process of retirement begins years before people actually retire from their jobs. Effective retirement planning needs to begin early in adulthood. Unfortunately, many Americans are faced with various financial pressures, such as mortgages and their children's college educations, during the same years in which they should be saving and investing for their own retirements. For people who fail to plan for retirement, Social Security may be their only source of income. In fact, for over half of all older adults in the United States, Social Security is the only source of income. For many of these people, Social Security fails to cover all of their needs. Many of these people are eligible for Supplemental Security Income (SSI), which provides payments to poor older people.

Another federal program intended to help older people is Medicare, which provides both medical and hospital insurance to people over 65. Although Medicare has benefited older Americans, it does not cover all of their medical needs, and uncovered expenses may be costly.

In addition to Social Security and Medicare, many older people are eligible for company pension benefits upon retirement. Some pension plans are based solely on individual employee contributions, others are paid for by the employer, and still others are based upon contributions from both the employee and the employer. Many people who are not covered by company plans may be able to set up Individual Retirement Accounts (IRAs).

Tragically, despite government programs and private pensions, the poverty rate among older people remains high. According to the Census Bureau, 12.2% of older adults lived below the poverty line in 1990, up from 11.4% in 1989. This rate was higher for women than men, and much higher for minorities than for whites. For older Hispanics, the rate of poverty was 28.1% in 1990; for older African-Americans, the rate was 31.9%.

Not surprisingly, income and health care issues are extremely important to older Americans, and there are a number of well-organized groups claiming to represent their interests. Perhaps the most influential of these groups is the American Association of Retired Persons (AARP), which had 32–33 million members in 1992. AARP lobbies Congress and state legislatures on a variety of issues relevant to the needs of older Americans.

Gerontologist Robert Atchley has noted that as people age they tend to become more active politically. The political predilections of older adults cover the entire political spectrum. However, they are more likely than younger voters to be concerned about Social Security, health care issues, tax increases, and inflation.

In addition to their participation in politics, older people often volunteer in their communities, in churches and synagogues, hospitals, schools, and a wide variety of other organizations. In an era of reduced state and federal programming, older volunteers help fill part of the void in social services. Volunteerism aids the community and provides a meaningful way for older people to work, help others, interact socially, and structure their days.

As people age, they are faced with many choices, but these choices are limited by resources. Older people maximize their choices through their decisions regarding work, retirement, financial planning, political involvement, and volunteer work.

DESCRIPTION OF ACTIVITIES

Congratulations, You're Retired!

One of the most significant transitions associated with later life is retirement. In this activity, learners are asked to assume the role of a married 65-year-old man who has recently retired as a sales manager of a large company. Learners also describe their own plans, expectations, and personal preferences for retirement based on their financial and health concerns.

Balancing the Fixed Income Budget

In this activity, learners develop a monthly budget for an older couple. Learners allocate funds to cover such expenses as food, clothing, utilities, health care, and recreation. After completing the budget process, learners describe the constraints associated with managing a budget on a fixed income.

Developing a Political Platform for Older Americans

In this activity, learners are asked to take on the role of political leaders or representatives of older American coalitions and prepare the planks of a national political platform. Policies on Social Security, tax reform, and health care are examined.

A Way to Spend My Days

In this activity, learners are presented with the case of two older adults who volunteer their time 6 days a week at a church that provides lunch for the homeless. Through group discussion, learners discuss the relationship between self-esteem and work. Learners also consider possible volunteer efforts in which they might wish to engage when they retire.

```
┌─────────────────────────────────┐
│         ┌──────────────┐         │
│         │   Activity   │         │
│         └──────────────┘         │
│                                  │
│   Congratulations, You're Retired! │
│                                  │
└─────────────────────────────────┘
```

PURPOSE

The purpose of this activity is to explore retirement as a role, preparation for retirement, and subsequent adjustment to retirement. Upon completion of this activity, the learner will be able to:

1. Describe the expectations, privileges, and personal requirements of being retired for two people, who are to be interviewed.

2. Discuss financial and health concerns that have a bearing on retirement.

3. Describe the retirement planning activities of the persons interviewed.

TIME REQUIRED

3 hours and 45 minutes (2 hours for the interviews, 1 hour to prepare summaries of the interviews, and 45 minutes to discuss the activity in class)

PROCEDURE

1. Learners interview two older adults who have retired from full-time employment.

2. Learners use the questions listed in the activity sheet as a guide for the interviews and to prepare one- or two-page summaries of each of the interviews.

3. The instructor leads a class discussion of the activity.

4. The instructor may lead a more general class discussion based on the following questions.

DISCUSSION QUESTIONS

1. Do you think you will want to continue to work past the age of 65? Explain.

2. Compare the responses of the two retired persons whom you interviewed.

3. What are the most common sources of income for retired persons?

4. In what ways can individuals become better prepared for retirement?

5. How might family roles change in relation to retirement?

6. What do you most look foward to regarding your own retirement?

Congratulations, You're Retired!

Interview two people who have retired from full-time employment. Ask each person to respond to the questions listed below. Following each of the interviews, prepare a one- or two-page summary of the subject's responses.

1. When did you retire?

2. When did you start planning your retirement?

3. In what ways did you plan financially?

4. What financial strategies would you recommend to people who are starting to plan for their retirement?

5. In what ways is your life different from when you were employed?

6. What do you most enjoy about retirement?

7. What do you least enjoy about retirement?

8. How has your retirement affected you relationships with family and friends?

9. How might your retirement be affected by your health?

10. Is your life in retirement what you expected it would be?

11. What recommendations do you have for younger adults as they begin to make plans for retirement?

```
┌─────────────────────────┐
│        Activity         │
└─────────────────────────┘

    Balancing the
  Fixed Income Budget
```

PURPOSE

The purpose of this activity is to help the learner appreciate the financial constraints faced by some older adults living on fixed incomes. Upon completion of this activity, the learner will be able to:

1. Construct a monthly budget for someone on a limited budget.

2. Describe the problems associated with living on a fixed income.

3. Discuss the economic status of older adults in American society.

TIME REQUIRED

1¹/₂ hours (1 hour to complete the activity sheet and 30 minutes to discuss the activity in class)

PROCEDURE

1. Learners complete the activity sheet individually.

2. Following completion of the activity sheets, the instructor divides the class into pairs. Learners discuss their responses to the activity sheet with their partners.

3. Following these discussions, the instructor leads a class discussion of the activity.

4. The instructor may lead a more general class discussion based on the following questions.

DISCUSSION QUESTIONS

1. What problems might interfere with using the budget that you constructed?

2. How does the financial status of older people compare to that of the rest of the population?

3. What are the most common sources of income for people over 65?

4. What are the strengths and weaknesses of the Social Security system?

5. How do most older Americans pay for health care?

Balancing the Fixed Income Budget

You are assigned the task of constructing a monthly budget for Darlene and Daniel Davis, a retired couple, both of whom are in their mid-70s. Their monthly after-tax income from Social Security, a pension, and an investment is $2,250. They have a savings account containing $12,000. They own their own home and a 1989 mid-sized automobile.

Below you will find various categories of expenses. Some of the categories have been completed. You are to complete the other expense categories. The total should not exceed the Davis's monthly income of $2,250.

Item	Amount budgeted
Auto insurance	$ 60.00
Auto repair	_____
Clothing	_____
Contributions to charity	_____
Cosmetics	_____
Electricity	100.00
Food	_____
Fuel (gas and oil for car)	_____
Health insurance	_____
Heating	_____
Home maintenance	_____
Homeowner's insurance	60.00
Household supplies	_____
Lawn care	_____
Life insurance	35.00
Loans or credit card payments	_____
Major purchases (new car, appliance)	_____
Medical expenses (medicines, doctor visits not covered by health insurance or Medicare)	_____

Item	Amount Budgeted
Property tax	*100.00*
Recreation	_____
Telephone	*40.00*
Water	*15.00*
Other	_____
Total	*$2,250.00*

Activity

Developing a Political Platform for Older Americans

PURPOSE
The purpose of this activity is to provide a framework for examining various political issues of interest to older Americans. Upon completion of this activity, the learner will be able to:

1. List several policy issues of interest to older people.

2. Analyze how Social Security and health care expenses affect older Americans.

TIME REQUIRED
45 minutes (25 minutes to discuss the activity sheet in groups and 20 minutes to discuss the activity sheet as a class)

PROCEDURE
1. The class is divided into groups of four to seven.

2. Each group completes the activity sheet.

3. Following completion of the activity sheets, each group presents its findings to the entire class.

4. Following these presentations, the instructor leads a discussion of the activity.

5. The instructor may lead a more general class discussion based on the following questions.

DISCUSSION QUESTIONS
1. What policy issues concern older people?

2. What are some of the most influential organizations representing the political interests of older people?

3. Are there voting patterns that differentiate older voters from younger ones?

4. Do you think that older persons form a voting block? Explain.

5. Are political activities among older persons likely to increase with the aging of America? Explain.

Developing a Political Platform for Older Americans

Your group has been asked to prepare a statement regarding several issues of interest to older residents of your state. Your group will be testifying before a public forum organized by the office of your state's governor. Your group represents a coalition of organizations expressing concerns about the needs of the older population. The task of your group is to develop a list of issues that you believe are of particular interest to older people and to describe possible changes that might reflect the needs of this group. As a group, prepare your political statement by focusing on two or three issues.

```
┌─────────────────────────────────────────────┐
│              ┌──────────────────┐            │
│              │    Activity      │            │
│              └──────────────────┘            │
│                                              │
│                                              │
│         A Way to Spend My Days               │
│                                              │
│                                              │
└─────────────────────────────────────────────┘
```

PURPOSE

The purpose of this activity is to prompt the learner to consider the benefits to older people of performing volunteer work. Upon completion of this activity, the learner will be able to:

1. Discuss the relationship between self-esteem and volunteer activities.

2. Describe some of the possible ways in which he or she might provide community service upon retirement.

TIME REQUIRED

45 minutes (15 minutes to discuss the activity sheet in groups, 15 minutes to present the findings to the class, and 15 minutes to discuss the activity as a class)

PROCEDURE

1. The class is divided into groups of three or four.

2. Each group reads the case and answers the questions at the end of the case.

3. Following completion of the activity sheets, each group presents its findings to the entire class.

4. Following these presentations, the instructor leads a discussion of the activity.

5. The instructor may lead a more general class discussion based on the following questions.

DISCUSSION QUESTIONS

1. Why is self-esteem so often tied to one's professional and leisure activities?

140

2. Some people view their older years as a time when they can do what they want. As an older adult, how would you most want to spend your days?

3. As an older adult, do you think you will enjoy volunteer work? Why or why not?

4. Why is paid work more valued in American society than most volunteer work?

A Way to Spend My Days

Read and analyze the case study and answer the questions that follow it.

LaVerne is tired, but she looks forward to each new day. Her life has taken on new meaning in the last 6 months. Since she and her sister, Thelma, decided to start the kitchen for the homeless, things have looked up for her. After her husband's death, LaVerne maintained an interest in church activities and in gardening, but overall, she felt kind of down. Now, 6 days a week, she rises each morning knowing she has the responsibility—and the joy—of cooking for the approximately 2 dozen persons who eat their noon—and maybe only—meal at LaVerne's church. Twenty years ago, LaVerne ran a small restaurant, and she is proud to be able to draw on that experience. LaVerne and Thelma are good cooks and they believe that what they are doing is a very good way to spend their days.

1. Why might LaVerne's self-esteem increase with her role of organizing and cooking for the homeless?

2. LaVerne is energetic and in good health. Suppose that she begins to slow down and feels that she can no longer provide this type of service. What other forms of human service could she provide?

3. Suppose that you are retired and that you are able to provide volunteer service in your community. What kinds of volunteer work would most appeal to you?

Chapter 8

Moving to a Long-Term Care Facility

FOR ALL PEOPLE, BUT PARTICULARLY FOR OLDER PEOPLE, RELOCATION IS A stressful event. Moving to a long-term care facility can be especially stressful. Relocation means parting with treasured keepsakes, one's home, one's neighborhood, one's friends. It is an acknowledgment that one phase of life has ended and another—final—phase has begun. It is thus common for older people entering long-term care facilities to face feelings of loss, fear, isolation, and confusion.

Entering a nursing home, a new resident is faced with an institutional setting and a congregate living environment. Prior to entering the nursing home, the resident may have been living alone, or with his or her spouse. Suddenly, the new resident must cope with living with dozens or even hundreds of people. The new resident may no longer have a room to him- or herself, but must get used to sharing a room with another person. Few personal items will fill the room, which will feel impersonal and institutional. Whereas previously the resident may have taken care of him- or herself, staff members will now be part of the new resident's life. Whereas previously the resident was free to engage in his or her own personal habits and routines, he or she must now operate according to the nursing home's schedule, so that the facility can accommodate the needs of all of its residents.

Although older adults entering a nursing home face many unpleasant changes, some feel relief over the move. For these older people, taking care of a home, shopping, and preparing meals becomes difficult, and there is a sense of relief over being able to relinquish these responsibilities. Most importantly, there is comfort in knowing that nursing and medical staff are available to deal with the resident's medical problems.

There are many ways in which long-term care facilities can try to minimize the negative aspects and emphasize the positive aspects of institutionalized care. One key to adjustment for residents of long-term care facilities is to maintain contact with friends and family. Family and friends should try to visit the resident frequently and include the resident in community activities, to the extent that the resident's health permits such participation. Care should be taken to give the resident as much control as possible. This means that the resident participates in the planning of his or her daily schedule. Residents should also be informed of decisions regarding their care. Finally, residents should stay active within the facility by taking advantage of the organized activities offered.

Both federal and state regulations protect the rights of residents of nursing facilities. These rights, known as the resident's bill of rights, are set forth in the activity sheet.

Caring for older adults can be a difficult job, and people who care for residents in long-term care facilities may become frustrated and take out their frustration on the residents. In some instances, this venting can take the form of abuse. Abuse of nursing home residents is illegal, and must be reported by anyone who witnesses or suspects such behavior. Signs that should arouse suspicion include physical evidence of abuse, such as bruises or cuts; sadness or depression on the part of the resident following a particular staff person's shift; excessive teasing of the resident by a staff member; and impatience or roughness by a staff member.

Another form of abuse is the unnecessary use of physical and chemical restraints. Physical restraints are wrist or chest devices that prevent a person from getting out of a chair or bed. In the past they have been used to restrain residents who tend to wander. Chemical restraints refer to the use of psychotropic medications to sedate people whose behavior is difficult to control. Federal regulations now prohibit the use of restraints unless they are necessary to prevent the resident from hurting him- or herself. They can no longer be used to make life easier for the staff of the facility.

A move to a long-term facility need not mean the end of an older person's individuality. Families and professionals must work to ensure that a high quality of life be maintained for nursing home residents, and that they continue to live in dignity.

DESCRIPTION OF ACTIVITIES

Welcome to Our Nursing Home: Facilitating Adjustment

In this activity, the trauma of relocation to a nursing home is explored. Following a traumatic accident and subsequent hospitalization, a resident is transferred to a nursing home for further care. Learners explore ways in which this transition can be facilitated for the patient, who opposed the move, and the family members, who supported the move. Learners also discuss possible alternative living arrangements.

Applying the Resident's Bill of Rights

This activity is designed for nursing home staff members or students of gerontology who wish to familiarize themselves with rights of residents of nursing facilities. By working individually and in groups, learners review the resident's rights and describe possible ways in which staff might interfere with the free exercise of these rights or facilitate promotion of these rights. Learners use case studies to determine which rights may have been violated, and are asked to describe appropriate actions and responses.

A Case of Abuse

In this activity, learners assume the role of a health care professional and discuss how they might respond to a possible case of abuse. Learners describe their methods of investigation and legal obligations, and addresss the ethical issues facing the health care professional under these circumstances.

The Ideal Nursing Home

In this activity, learners are asked to design an ideal nursing home, including constructing a purpose and philosophy of care, a suggested management style, and a diagram of the facility.

Welcome to Our Nursing Home: Facilitating Adjustment

PURPOSE

The purpose of this activity is to familiarize the learner with the changes experienced by older adults following a move to a nursing home. The activity focuses on adjustment patterns and feelings that are central to translocation. Upon completion of this activity, the learner will be able to:

1. Cite some of the changes associated with moving to a nursing home.

2. Describe his or her own feelings about becoming unable to live independently.

TIME REQUIRED

40 minutes (20 minutes to complete the activity sheet and 20 minutes to discuss the activity in class)

PROCEDURE

1. The class is divided into groups of five to seven.

2. Each group reads the case study and answers the questions at the end of the case.

3. Each group chooses one person to record and present its findings to the entire class.

4. The instructor leads a class discussion of the activity.

5. The instructor may lead a more general class discussion based on the following questions.

DISCUSSION QUESTIONS

1. How might one's self-concept be altered by living in a nursing home?

2. How can family members assist in the decision to relocate to a nursing home and the relocation process?

3. What significant stressors might have an impact upon a person who is moving into a nursing home?

4. How can nursing home personnel assist in the facilitation of adjustment to the nursing home?

Welcome to Our Nursing Home: Facilitating Adjustment

Read and analyze the case study and answer the questions that follow it.

Mr. Johnson is a single, 89-year-old male, who is alert and in good health. Although he was deeply saddened by his wife's death 5 years ago, he adjusted well to her death.

Mr. Johnson has three children, two daughters and a son. One of his daughters lives in San Francisco and the other one lives in Washington, D.C. His son lives in a nearby suburb and has recently remarried.

Mr. Johnson continues to drive his car and attends senior activities on a regular basis. He also continues to take daily walks. He has been able to maintain his home with the assistance of a housekeeper who comes in 4 hours each week. His son accompanies him to the grocery store during his weekly visits.

Yesterday, while on his evening walk, Mr. Johnson fell and was unable to get back on his feet. He yelled for help. A neighbor heard his plea and called for emergency help. Mr. Johnson was taken to the local hospital where he was diagnosed with a fractured hip and taken to surgery.

His son, Ben, is concerned about how his father will manage following discharge from the hospital. Will he need more assistance? Will he be able to live alone? Will he need to go to a nursing home? Ben and his father had often talked about his father going to a nursing home, and Ben knows his father is very much opposed to such a move. Ben is waiting for the doctor's report and wondering how his life and his father's life may change.

Five days after surgery, Mr. Johnson was making progress toward recovery. He was transferred from the hospital to a nursing home. Nursing home staff members took Mr. Johnson to his room and were ready to assist with the adjustment surrounding the move.

1. What alternative living arrangements could have been used in this case?

2. Assume that Mr. Johnson needed to be placed in a nursing home on a temporary basis following his surgery.

    a. What factors should Mr. Johnson's family consider in selecting a nursing home?

    b. What preparations need to be made?

    c. What feelings do you experience as you plan your strategy for moving Mr. Johnson to a nursing home?

Applying the Resident's Bill of Rights

PURPOSE

The purpose of this activity is to make the learner aware of the basic rights guaranteed to all nursing home residents. Upon completion of this activity, the learner will be able to:

1. Identify the rights of nursing home residents, as mandated by federal and state regulations.

2. Describe the ways that nursing home staff interfere with residents' ability to exercise their rights.

3. Describe ways that nursing home staff can facilitate the exercise of resident rights.

TIME REQUIRED

1¹/₂ hours (1 hour to complete the activity sheet and 30 minutes to discuss the activity in class)

PROCEDURE

1. Learners review the list of residents' rights included in the activity sheet.

2. Learners read each case study and determine which right is being violated.

3. Learners discuss the appropriate action or response to each case study.

4. The instructor leads a class discussion of the activity.

5. The instructor may lead a more general class discussion based on the following questions.

DISCUSSION QUESTIONS

1. Why are residents' rights so important?

2. Do you know of any nursing home practices that may have led to the formal establishment of these rights? Explain.

3. Which of these rights would be most important to you if you were a nursing home resident?

4. Why might some nursing home administrators and staff resist the implementation of some of these rights?

The Resident's Bill of Rights[1]

Each resident in a nursing home has a right to:

1. Be informed and have a written copy of the resident's rights and responsibilities.

2. Exercise rights as a resident of the facility and a citizen of the United States.

3. Be free from discrimination, interference, and reprisal in the exercise of these rights.

4. Inspect his or her own medical records.

5. Be informed of his or her health status and medical condition.

6. Refuse treatment and refuse to participate in experimental research.

7. Be informed about services available and related charges, including information about coverage under the Medicare and Medicaid programs.

8. Have his or her family and physician notified promptly when there is a change in condition.

9. Be notified in a reasonable time frame of any changes in room assignment, roommate, transfer, and discharge.

10. Manage his or her own financial affairs.

11. Choose his or her attending physician.

12. Participate in his or her care and treatment.

13. Be granted privacy in accommodations; medical treatment; meetings with friends, family, and/or resident groups; written and telephone communications; and conjugal visits.

14. Have his or her personal and clinical records kept confidential.

---

[1]*Code of Federal Regulations,* No. 42, Part 483, Subpart B: "Requirements for Long Term Facilities." § 483.10, 483.12, 483.13, 483.15, 1991.

15. Voice grievances and file complaints without discrimination, coercion, or reprisal.

16. Examine survey results.

17. Refuse to perform services for the facility.

18. Send and receive mail.

19. Receive visitors, including relatives, representatives from the state, and the area ombudsman.

20. Have regular access and private use of a telephone.

21. Retain and use personal possessions as space permits.

22. Share a room with his or her spouse.

23. Self-administer drugs, unless this is determined to be an unsafe procedure.

24. Be free from restraints.

25. Be free from abuse.

26. Choose activities, schedules, and health care consistent with his or her own interests and plan for care.

27. Participate in social, religious, and community activities and interact with people of his or her own choosing.

28. Receive services and care with reasonable accommodation of individual preferences.

Applying the Resident's Bill of Rights

The following cases represent situations that one may encounter as a staff member in a nursing home. Read each case. Then use the Resident's Bill of Rights to determine which right is being violated. Determine what actions you would take to protect and ensure the rights of the resident in each situation.

1. Mr. and Mrs. Harold Inrick have been married for 40 years. They recently entered a nursing home, because they are no longer able to cook or take care of their home. Mr. Inrick has been ill and was placed in the section of the nursing home for more acute residents. Mrs. Inrick has a room on the second floor, and expects her husband to be placed in the room after he has recovered from his illness. Mrs. Inrick visits her husband frequently. One day the nursing assistant walks into the room and finds Mr. and Mrs. Inrick in bed together.

2. Mrs. Sally Renner has been in the Valley View Nursing Home for 5 years. She is alert and active in the resident council. She asks the nurse about the new medication her doctor has ordered. The nurse responds: "Don't worry about it dear, the doctor knows what's best."

3. When Mrs. Opal Hanna entered the nursing home, she entrusted her Social Security check, her savings, and her small pension to the administrator of the home. She gets a weekly allowance to buy essentials and other things she needs. One day, Mrs. Hanna asked to see the records of how her money had been spent and to determine how much savings she had left. The administrator refused to share these records, assuring Mrs. Hanna that her money was secure and that there was plenty of money to provide for her care.

4. Mr. John Young is an 81-year-old resident of Park View Methodist Home. Since entering the facility at the age of 78, he has been a chronic complainer. Yesterday he asked the nurse supervisor how he

can register a complaint about the treatment at the nursing home. She ignored him, realizing that he has always been unhappy and really doesn't know what he wants anyway.

5. Betty Jackson and Chantelle White, two nursing assistants at Riverside Convalescent, are talking in the hall about Mr. Peng, the new resident in Room 504. They laugh about the way he walks and complain about how demanding he is.

6. Ms. Nettie Jones was being assisted with her daily hygiene. Nursing assistant Sophie Johnson was very carefully bathing Nettie. The door to the room was open and the curtain was not pulled. Nettie's exposed body could be seen from the hallway.

7. Joe Smith arrived at Shady Lane Nursing Home after carefully deciding this was the best living arrangement for him. Joe had scheduled his interview with the admissions director. After 4 days at Shady Lane, Joe has some concerns over some aspects of his care. He is wondering what his rights are. He begins asking about his rights. He thought he was to have received a copy. He's told, "We'll get you a copy." After 6 days, he still does not have a copy of his rights.

8. Emmett Jones arranged for his family physician, Dr. Allen, to see him while he was in the nursing home. He brought with him an envelope containing medical orders and a statement from the nursing home's physician, Dr. White, confirming that Dr. Allen could continue to provide medical care and treatment for Emmett in the nursing home. Nurse Sandy Wilcox informs Emmett that Dr. White must provide all medical care for Emmett while he is at Shady Lane, and that Dr. Allen can treat him only upon his release from the facility.

9. Dr. Moran wrote orders for Mrs. Elisa Mills to self-administer her medications. Nurse Nancy Johnson informs Mrs. Mills that nurses are the only people that hand out medications at Seton Presbyterian and that self-administration of medications is in strict violation of Seton's policies.

10. One of Morris' biggest worries about entering a nursing home is his wife, Alice. He knows Alice is going to miss him. He hopes that a neighbor will be able to bring her to see him. She needs a ride to the nursing home and can only visit at certain times. Morris had discussed this with the admissions director. Now the staff tell him that his wife can visit only between the hours of 1 P.M. and 5 P.M. and that he and his wife must remain in the public nursing area.

11. Lou Michelson has asked the staff about being allowed to use the telephone. He is told that the phones are for business use only.

12. Bruce Hamilton planned to attend the Resident Council Meeting on Tuesday morning. He told the day nurse of his plan at breakfast that morning. The meeting was to begin at 9 A.M. Just before 9, the nursing assistant informed Bruce that she was ready to give him his bath. Bruce informed Sue of his plan and she replied, "You'll miss your bath if you go." Bruce knows that the bath schedule calls for only one bath per week.

13. Three weeks after entering Crest View Nursing Center, Robert Max is beginning to feel like an alien. He brought his favorite stuffed animal with him, a source of security and comfort. When the nursing assistant noticed the animal, she informed Robert that he was not allowed to have stuffed toys and that if she saw the toy again, she would confiscate it.

14. Lou Maccini has been at Shady Lane Nursing Home for 6 weeks. He has received no mail, although he has written to his children and friends regularly. One day his daughter calls to talk to him. She asks how he liked the letters and pictures his grandchildren had sent him. "What letters?" he wonders.

15. Elsie Jefferson notices that one of the residents is always in a special chair near the nurses' station. She seems to be tied up most of the time. When she asks the nurse why the resident is always tied up, she is told the woman is too confused to wander around the nursing home by herself.

```
                    ┌──────────────┐
                    │   Activity   │
                    └──────────────┘

                A Case of Abuse
```

PURPOSE

The purpose of this activity is to familiarize the learner with aspects of care that may lead to frustration and possible abuse. Upon completion of this activity, the learner will be able to:

1. Define abuse.

2. Identify key factors that may lead to an abusive situation.

TIME REQUIRED

45 minutes (25 minutes to complete the activity sheet and 20 minutes to discuss the activity in class)

PROCEDURE

1. The class is divided into groups of three to four.

2. Each group reads the case study and discusses the questions that follow the case.

3. Each group selects a spokesperson to present the group's findings to the entire class.

4. The instructor leads a class discussion that integrates the ideas generated by each group.

5. The instructor may lead a more general class discussion based on the following questions.

DISCUSSION QUESTIONS

1. What are some possible indications that abuse has taken place?

2. What factors may lead to abuse in the institutional setting?

3. What factors may lead to abuse in a family context?

4. What behaviors are frequently seen following abuse?

5. What are some of the emotional reactions that are exhibited following episodes of abuse?

A Case of Abuse

In your group, discuss the following case and construct a group response to the discussion questions.

"Minnie has a mean streak. She sure does. Look at the scratches she gave me when I placed her in the whirlpool on Friday. I bet she gave them hell when she was young," smiled the nursing assistant. "I really got her back, though. She won't do anything to me again. Giving her a bath will be a breeze from now on."

Ellen, the charge nurse, overheard these comments as she passed the room where the nursing assistants were taking their break. Ellen stopped sharply, stunned and dazed by what she had just heard.

Ellen was on the way to visit Minnie. Minnie's daughter, Alice, had requested that Ellen speak with Minnie. Alice had expressed concerns that something was different about her mother. Since Ellen had known Minnie for some time, Alice thought Ellen would be able to determine if anything was wrong with Minnie.

Ellen knocked on Minnie's door and entered. She found Minnie sitting in her favorite chair, holding her special teddy bear. Minnie barely looked up at the sound of Ellen's voice. Her usual greeting was to reach out her arms, and take Ellen's hand in her own. Then she would look up, smile, and kiss Ellen's hand.

Ellen stood quietly, saying nothing. Slowly, Ellen moved toward Minnie. Ellen placed a chair near Minnie and quietly sat down beside her.

Ellen recalled the signs and symptoms of abuse: sudden changes in behavior; unwillingness to talk; unjustified fear or suspicion; bruises, swelling, untreated injuries, and fractures; and inappropriate clothing. She also recalled that victims of abuse often internalize blame, experience guilt, behave passively, remain socially isolated, and display loyalty toward the assaulter out of fear of loss or additional harm. Fear of additional harm and other factors often prevent abused people from reporting the abuse.

1. If you were Ellen, how would you respond to Minnie?
    a. What would you say?

    b. What nonverbal responses would you use?

2. Is Minnie exhibiting typical signs of having been abused?

3. What other signs or symptoms are observed in victims of abuse?

4. What approaches will Ellen use to intervene with Minnie?

5. What will Ellen tell Alice, Minnie's daughter?

6. What behavioral characteristics of abuse are being voiced by the nursing assistant?

7. Who will investigate the situation with the nursing assistant?

8. Are there any legal obligations to fulfill in this situation?

9. What are the moral and ethical responsibilities of someone who suspects abuse?

```
┌─────────────────────────────────┐
│        ┌──────────────┐         │
│        │   Activity    │         │
│        └──────────────┘         │
│                                  │
│    The Ideal Nursing Home        │
│                                  │
└─────────────────────────────────┘
```

PURPOSE

The purpose of this activity is to prompt the learner to think about what constitutes an ideal nursing home. Upon completion of this activity, the learner will be able to:

1. Identify features of an ideal nursing home.

2. Identify factors that should determine nursing home design and management.

TIME REQUIRED

$2^1/_2$ hours (2 hours to complete the activity sheet and 30 minutes to discuss the activity in class)

PROCEDURE

1. Learners complete the activity sheet as a homework assignment.

2. Following completion of the activity sheets, the instructor divides the class into pairs. Learners discuss their responses to the activity sheet with their partners.

3. Following the small group discussion, the instructor leads a class discussion that integrates the ideas generated by the learners.

4. The instructor may lead a more general class discussion based on the following questions.

DISCUSSION QUESTIONS

1. Which design features are basic to an ideal nursing home?

2. What special characteristics are to be incorporated in the governing of an ideal nursing home?

3. What do residents want in a nursing home?

4. How can the needs and desires of residents, as well as staff be incorporated in the ideal nursing home?

The Ideal Nursing Home

Land on which to build the nursing home is available. Money, contractors, and the necessary supplies are at your disposal. You have no constraints—you have been given total freedom to design and build an ideal nursing home.

Be creative in designing the ideal nursing home. Perhaps it is the nursing home that you will one day enter.

1. Develop a purpose and a philosophy of care for the facility.

2. Describe the management style that will be implemented.

3. Draw a diagram showing the physical design of an ideal nursing home. Include the following components: resident rooms, central bathing area, dining room, activity room, nurses' station, family visiting areas, lobby, and administrative offices.

4. Indicate reasons for the location of various areas included in your design (traffic patterns, visual access by nursing staff, privacy, distance between work areas).

Chapter 9

Death and Dying

LIKE BIRTH, DEATH IS A NATURAL PART OF LIFE, A UNIVERSAL EVENT WITHIN the life of each person. This chapter examines attitudes toward death and dying and ways in which people deal with grieving and surviving.

Death means different things to different people, and attitudes toward old age and death vary widely. These attitudes are affected by culture, religion, and life experiences. Although death is no longer the taboo subject it once was, many people feel uncomfortable discussing death. Fear of the unknown, fear of loneliness, fear of pain, fear of loss of identity, and fear of loss of control all arise when one thinks about dying. A component of dealing with death and dying is coping with these fears.

Changes in medical technology have prompted many people to think about how they will die. Technology has forced us to think deeply about how much assistance we want merely to stay alive. Questions about quality of life that were unthinkable a generation ago have now become almost routine. The Patient Self-Determination Act legislates that patients be informed of their right to prepare an *advance directive*. An advance directive can be a living will or a durable power of attorney for health care. A living will is a document in which a person states whether he or she wants to be provided artificial life support in the event that he or she becomes terminally ill and cannot express his or her preferences. A durable power of attorney for health care is a document that directs a designated individual to make decisions for the person if he or she cannot make those decisions. Authority to provide treatments can be made by the persons designated in the durable power of attorney. Rules regarding living wills and durable powers of attorney vary from state to state. In some states, it is possible to prepare a single document describing treatment choices and designating another individual to act on one's behalf in healthcare decisions.

As people grow older, they begin to lose friends and family members to death. Many meaningful events of our lives are shared with others. With the death of friends and family members, a portion of one's own life thus ends. Death causes one to reflect on important events that were shared with the deceased person. Reflecting upon these memories often finalizes the reality of a loved one's death.

Grieving is the process of adapting to these losses. It involves both letting go and moving forward. Grieving takes time and often is worked through in stages. The first phase of this process is often denial, followed by anger, bargaining, depression, and finally, acceptance. Not everyone experiences all of these stages, and these stages are not always experienced in this order. It is nevertheless often useful to think about these stages when dealing with a person who is grieving.

DESCRIPTION OF ACTIVITIES

Contemplating Endings

Perceptions of mortality may change with age. This activity provides learners with the opportunity to examine their earlier recollections of death. Learners recall experiences with death, the ritualization of death, and perceptions of their own mortality. Learners may explore feelings of anxiety regarding death, which are best dealt with if the educator has set the stage for such a personal topic. This activity may not be appropriate for all learners, and is most effective when used in small classes.

Dealing with Death

In this activity, the final stage of life is portrayed as one of growth. Learners examine the case of Mrs. Angell, who is aware of her failing body and mind. Through this activity, learners examine their attitudes toward death, verbalize feelings about death and dying, and describe the place of fear and grief in the process of death.

Grieving and Surviving

This activity serves as a follow-up to the previous activity. The learners use a case study to analyze the reactions of Mrs. Angell's family in coping with her death. Learners explore the need for grief, look at variations of the grief process, and consider the nature of delayed grief. Learners are asked to consider mourning and grief as necessary functions in restructuring one's life following the death of a loved one. Instructors are advised that some learners may have difficulty in dealing with some of the emotional issues involved in the activity.

The Ethics of Dying

Through the use of case studies, this activity raises questions about several issues related to dying, including the right to die, the use of extraordinary means to keep a person alive, and euthanasia. Learners are asked to make choices in response to these hypothetical situations.

```
┌─────────────────────────┐
│      Activity           │
└─────────────────────────┘

     Contemplating Endings
```

PURPOSE

The purpose of this activity is to prompt the learner to recall his or her early recollections of death. Upon completion of this activity, the learner will be able to:

1. Examine his or her own responses to the issues of living and dying.

2. Understand the emotions that surround death and dying.

TIME REQUIRED

50 minutes (25 minutes to discuss the activity sheet with a partner and 25 minutes to discuss the activity as a class)

PROCEDURE

1. All learners select partners with whom they feel comfortable discussing death and dying.

2. Each pair of learners completes the activity sheet.

3. The instructor leads a class discussion of the activity.

4. The instructor may lead a more general class discussion based on the following questions.

DISCUSSION QUESTIONS

1. At what chronological ages do you think death is more easily accepted?

2. Elaborate on the statement, "We tend to deny death in our society."

3. Discuss possible reasons for a renewed interest in the topic of death.

4. How do the rituals surrounding death allow us to cope with our anxieties surrounding the reality of death?

Contemplating Endings

1. Recall your earliest recollections of death.
   a. How old were you?

   b. Who was the person who died?

   c. Who informed you of the person's death?

   d. How were you told?

   e. Where were you told?

   f. What did death mean to you at that time?

   g. Did learning of this person's death frighten you?

2. Was this person's death ritualized?
   a. How?

b. Did you attend the ceremony?

c. Was expression of grief allowed at the ceremony?

3. How old were you when you next encountered death? Were your feelings different from those you experienced the first time you learned about death?

4. Have you ever been with a terminally ill person? What emotions did you experience?

5. Let's say you could choose the time and circumstances surrounding your own death.
    a. At what age would you die?

    b. What would be the cause of death?

    c. Would death be slow or sudden?

    d. Would you speak openly about your death?

    e. Who would help you in finalizing your affairs?

    f. How would you wish to be remembered?

```
┌─────────────────────────────┐
│         ┌──────────┐         │
│         │ Activity │         │
│         └──────────┘         │
│                              │
│      Dealing with Death      │
│                              │
└─────────────────────────────┘
```

PURPOSE

The purpose of this activity is to prompt the learner to think about death as a natural process. Upon completion of this activity the learner will be able to:

1. Verbalize his or her feelings about death.

2. Recognize the need for expressing grief.

TIME REQUIRED

45 minutes (25 minutes to complete the activity sheet and 20 minutes to discuss the activity in pairs and as a class)

PROCEDURE

1. Learners complete the activity sheet individually.

2. Following completion of the activity sheets, the instructor divides the class into pairs. Learners discuss their responses to the activity sheet with their partners.

3. Following these discussions, the instructor leads a class discussion of the activity.

4. The instructor may lead a more general class discussion based on the following questions.

DISCUSSION QUESTIONS

1. How are issues related to death and dying usually dealt with in our society?

2. If you were faced with knowing that your death was imminent in the near future, what would matter most to you? Would you live differently?

Dealing with Death

Read and analyze the case study and answer the questions that follow it.

Mrs. Angell is 92 years old. She is aware that her mind and body are failing. She can no longer perform tasks as she once did. Mrs. Angell lives with her daughter, Rosa, and Rosa's family. She especially enjoys Anna, her grandchild.

In a recent visit to the doctor's office, Dr. Doe explained to Mrs. Angell that her condition was terminal. Mrs. Angell told Dr. Doe that she did not want to be hospitalized, and that she intended to live the remainder of her life at home with her family.

Mrs. Angell's hour of death arrived with her family near her. The moment of death was scarcely discernible as she quietly drew in her last breath and slowly exhaled. Anna was holding her grandmother's hand as her grasp loosened.

1. With your partner, role play the case, with one partner playing Mrs. Angell and the other playing Anna.

2. Discuss with your partner feelings that surfaced as you were enacting your role. Were you able to tell each other those things you wished to say? Were you able to say goodbye? What was your greatest fear?

3. If time permits, reverse the roles you played. Did you feel differently about death in the role of the other? Relate to your partner the feelings that you experienced.

Activity

Grieving and Surviving

PURPOSE

The purpose of this activity is to reveal to the learner the value of grieving. Upon completion of this activity the learner will be able to:

1. Acknowledge the need for expressing grief.

2. Recognize that grief may be delayed and may be a factor in another illness.

TIME REQUIRED

45 minutes (20 minutes to complete the activity sheet and 25 minutes to discuss the activity in class)

PROCEDURE

1. The class is divided into pairs.

2. Each pair of students completes the activity sheet.

3. Following completion of the activity sheets, the instructor leads a class discussion of the activity.

4. The instructor may lead a more general discussion based on the following questions.

DISCUSSION QUESTIONS

1. What do you consider as effective expressions of grieving? Are you comfortable with expressions of grief? What are your responses to such expressions?

2. Does time heal grief?

3. Elaborate on the statement, "The goal of grief work is not to avoid or eliminate painful feelings." How does one become comfortable with negative feelings?

4. Give suggestions for restructuring life following a death, releasing the person who has died, and moving on with one's own life. How long does this process take?

5. Can delayed grief be expressed as illness?

Grieving and Surviving

Read and analyze the case study and answer the questions that follow it.

Mrs. Angell was 92 years old when she died. She had lived with her family for several years prior to her death and they were very close. Following her death, her family began the long process of grieving. Her absence leaves a void, and they know they must mourn. Individually and personally, each member begins the path of mourning.

Mrs. Angell had recognized that death was a natural part of life. She was a model to her family, in that after living a long life, she had been ready for the final moment. Mrs. Angell had always been able to express her feelings and had spoken to the family often about death and how things would be after her death.

All of her family realize that Mrs. Angell lived a long life and had peacefully resolved the meaning of her life. Sometimes, the family members feel guilty because they are not able to let go as peacefully as she did. Perhaps they are thinking of themselves and realizing they were cheated from being able to spend more time with their loved one.

Sometimes when family members come home, it is as though Mrs. Angell were still in the house. It is easy to deny that she is gone. The relationship that the family had with Mrs. Angell took a long time to build. Restructuring of a new life without her will also take time.

The family decided they would enable each other to deal with their sorrow and mental anguish. They acknowledged that each member's style of grieving depends on each person's personality and the relationship that person shared with Mrs. Angell.

Since it is the first few weeks when separation is most keenly felt, family members decided they would gather together with relatives each week for sharing and support. Several months after the death, restructuring of time, personal goals, living space arrangements, and new patterns of living are finally beginning to come together.

1. How did Mrs. Angell's family deal with her death?

2. How would the grief process be different for Mrs. Angell's grandchildren and her adult children?

3. What other methods might have been used to cope with death?

4. What methods have you used to deal with death?

5. Is the grieving process affected by the circumstances of death (accidental, terminal illness, homicide, suicide)? Explain.

```
┌─────────────────────┐
│      Activity        │
└─────────────────────┘


    The Ethics of Dying
```

PURPOSE

The purpose of this activity is to allow the learner to examine his or her own beliefs regarding the ethics of dying. Upon completion of this activity, the learner will be able to:

1. State some of the controversial issues surrounding dying, including the right to die and the right to reject extraordinary means of life support.

2. Evaluate personal beliefs concerning the ethical dilemmas surrounding dying.

TIME REQUIRED

1 hour (30 minutes to complete the activity and 30 minutes to discuss the activity in class)

PROCEDURE

1. Learners complete the activity sheet individually.

2. Following completion of the activity sheets, the instructor leads a class discussion of the activity.

3. The instructor may lead a more general class discussion based on the following questions.

DISCUSSION QUESTIONS

1. What is the difference between passive and active euthanasia?

2. How does the notion of informed consent apply to the dying?

3. Would you consider setting up a living will for yourself? Why or why not?

4. What is the proper role of families in deciding the extent of treatment for a dying person who is comatose?

The Ethics of Dying

Prepare written responses to the following questions.

1. Following a heart attack, your 75-year-old father is in a coma. The attending physician does not expect him to recover. What would you do?

2. Would your decision be different if your father were 50?

3. Let's suppose the situation is different. Instead of heart problems, your 75-year-old father is suffering from inoperable bone cancer. He is alert and aware of his pain. He tells you that he wishes to die. Does he have the right to choose to die?

4. Who should decide if and when death is preferable to life—the patient, the patient's family, or the attending physician?

5. Your 85-year-old mother has been recuperating from a stroke. She has been nourished and hydrated with intravenous fluids and naso-gastric tube feedings. You understand that her capacity to swallow will most likely be permanently impaired. You are asked to give consent for the permanent placement of a gastrostomy tube in her stomach for feeding purposes. Your mother is unable to communicate her desires. However, in earlier years, she clearly stated that she did not wish to be kept alive by extraordinary means. What would you do?

Chapter 10

Issues for Professional Caregivers

WORKING WITH OLDER ADULTS AND THEIR FAMILIES CAN PROVIDE MANY rewards for the professional caregiver. Allied health professionals are often drawn to geriatric work by the promise of being able to make a positive difference in the lives of their clients.

An individual's values affect his or her choice of vocation. Psychologist Marguerite Kermis identifies a set of ideal values for health care personnel, including:

1. A commitment to the dignity of the individual
2. Respect for the individual and his or her uniqueness
3. A desire to maximize a person's functional capacities
4. A desire to work cooperatively on a continuing basis with an older person who is frail and vulnerable
5. A commitment to bear responsibility for the overall well-being of people who are mentally infirm
6. A commitment to deal with people honestly
7. A commitment to act on behalf of a person with diminished capabilities in accordance with that person's values, history, and lifestyle.[1]

Sometimes geriatric professionals face ethical dilemmas when two or more of their personal beliefs appear to be in conflict with one another. For example, a nurse may find it necessary to confront a client over what she considers to be an inappropriate behavior while worrying that the confrontation may prove threatening to the client's dignity and sense of autonomy.

Such dilemmas may come into play when working with family members of older clients. Sometimes family members make demands on geriatric professionals that appear to be in conflict with the best interests of the client, or that reflect underlying psychological problems of the family member rather than the needs of the client. Some family members com-

---

[1]Kermis, M. (1986). *Mental health in life: The adaptive process.* Monterey, CA: Jones and Bartlett, pp. 332–333.

plain about even the very best of service. Nursing home staff are confronted with some family members who are angry, fearful, conflicted, and guilt ridden; these emotions often erupt in the presence of nursing home staff. Certainly, concerns raised by family members need to be addressed, but some complaints stem from long-standing family and individual dysfunction.

Since the family accounts for so much interaction and social support for older people, the professional caregiver winds up serving the family as well as the aging client. Some of these families bring psychological problems that were unresolved in earlier development periods. Some parent–child conflicts that began with the birth of the child may continue and take on very different forms throughout the life cycle. The over-controlling parent may behave differently now that his or her child is an adult, but may nevertheless continue to try to manage that child's life. An angry son may continue to resent his father, although he may express that resentment in ways very different from when he was a rebellious adolescent. Children as well as spouses may mask their anger with guilt, and their guilt may lead them to overcompensate and do too much for their relatives. Spouses may resent the extra burdens of caring for a husband or wife with a disability; the resulting anger may also be connected to problems that began very early in the marriage.

Working with older people and their families can create a great deal of stress for the professional caregiver. Health educator Jerrold Greenberg describes several aspects of a job role that may create stress. These include role overload, role underload, role insufficiency, role ambiguity, and role conflict. Geriatrics professionals experience overload when there are too many demands placed upon them; they experience underload when a job is insufficiently demanding or fails to draw on the skills the job holder possesses. Role insufficiency occurs when an individual lacks experience or the specific skills to accomplish a task. Role ambiguity characterizes a work situation in which the expectations are unclear. Finally, role conflict occurs when an employee is caught between differing demands.

Psychologist Richard Lazarus and his colleagues suggest that the chronic stresses of life are more detrimental to a person than the more major life crises, which occur less frequently. In addition, Lazarus contends that ongoing positive experiences can counter the effects of chronic stress.

Professional caregivers may benefit greatly from a variety of stress management strategies in their efforts to cope with the demands of their work roles and personal lives. Numerous stress management tactics have been developed that focus on exercise, diet, meditation, relaxation, imagery, biofeedback, conflict resolution, assertion training, and time management.

Sometimes professional caregivers are overwhelmed by the stressors of their work and personal lives, which may result in a state of burnout. Greenberg describes several common symptoms of burnout:

- A diminished sense of humor
- An increase in physical complaints, such as fatigue and muscle tension
- Social withdrawal
- Loss of effectiveness at work
- Substance abuse
- Loss of self-esteem
- Emotional exhaustion
- Chronic frustration

Because of the heavy emotional—and in some cases physical—demands placed upon professional caregivers, burnout is a very common phenomenon. Professional caregivers are advised to share their concerns with friends and family, to secure time to engage in hobbies or other uplifting activies, to employ some workable form of time management, to choose to assert themselves when appropriate, to practice good personal health behaviors, and if all else fails, to consider the possibility of a change in work roles.

DESCRIPTION OF ACTIVITIES

Working with a Problem Family Member

This activity centers on a case study involving the daughter of a nursing home resident, who believes her mother is being neglected by the staff. Learners take on the role of the facility's social worker, and use a problem-solving approach to deal with the needs of both the daughter and the mother. Dysfunctional families often bring their conflicts to geriatric facilities. This learning experience looks at how professional caregivers can learn to cope with familial conflict, while trying to manage the care of the resident.

Stress Management for the Professional Caregiver

In this activity, learners are provided with the opportunity to examine personal stressors and begin the development of individualized stress management programs. Professional caregivers (nurses, social workers, nursing assistants, rehabilitation specialists) may experience a great deal of chronic stress in attempting to create a balance between the demands of their personal and professional lives. Learners are asked to list chronic stressors and personal reactions to those stressors. Following the development of this list, learners create guidelines for a stress management plan, including specifics on time management, assertiveness, exercise, and leisure activities.

The Case of the Caring Professional

In this activity, learners are introduced to an employee who is overinvolved with her clients. Such involvement often results in feelings of anxiety. Learners are asked to assume the role of the caring professional and share experiences they may have had professionally.

┌─────────────┐
│ Activity   │
└─────────────┘

Working with a
Problem Family Member

PURPOSE
The purpose of this activity is to allow the learner to analyze family dynamics. Upon completion of this activity, the learner will be able to:

1. Apply a family systems model to understanding a family conflict.

2. Use problem-solving methods to define family member conflicts.

3. Plan for resolution of conflicts within dysfunctional family systems.

TIME REQUIRED
45 minutes (25 minutes to complete the activity sheet and 20 minutes to discuss the activity in class)

PROCEDURE
1. The class is divided into groups of four to six.

2. Each group reads the case study and prepares written answers to the questions that follow the case study.

3. After all groups have completed the activity sheet, each group shares its responses with the entire class.

4. The instructor leads a class discussion that identifies themes emerging from these responses.

5. The instructor may lead a more general class discussion based on the following questions.

DISCUSSION QUESTIONS
1. What are several characteristics that distinguish functional from dysfunctional families?

2. Can family systems be "crazy"? How?

3. Why might intergenerational families resist efforts for positive change?

4. How do families use "scapegoating" of family members?

5. What types of difficulties can conflicted families present to nursing home, hospital, or home health staff?

Read and analyze the case study and answer the questions that follow it.

Wanda Merdoc, a frail 85-year-old widow, resides at Shady View Nursing Home. She is ambulatory with the help of a walker, but seems to prefer to stay in her room and talk to her roommate, Myra Cardin. Mrs. Merdoc has been a resident at the facility for the past year. She entered the facility following hospitalization for a fractured hip. She has slowly but steadily declined since her arrival.

Mrs. Merdoc's daughter, Glenda Moore, is convinced that her mother is being neglected. She tells the staff, "Mother just keeps looking bad. Why don't you take care of her?" Mrs. Moore can be downright nasty, screaming at the staff and demanding that they take care of her mother.

At the request of the facility's director of nursing, Ms. Zeel, the social worker, has set up a meeting with Mrs. Moore. Ms. Zeel is worried about this meeting. After all, last month Mrs. Moore called Ms. Zeel on the telephone and screamed at her.

1. If you were Ms. Zeel, how would you approach the problem?

2. How would you gather information regarding the problem?

3. Who should be involved in developing a solution to the problem?

4. Would an educational intervention be helpful in working with Mrs. Moore? Explain.

5. If you were Ms. Zeel, what suggestions would you offer to the nursing staff for dealing with Mrs. Merdoc and Mrs. Moore?

Stress Management
for the Professional Caregiver

PURPOSE

The purpose of this activity is to allow the learner to examine stressors and to develop a personalized stress management program. Upon completion of this activity, the learner will be able to:

1. Describe stress/distress scenarios encountered in daily living.

2. Analyze behavioral, emotional, and physical reactions to stressors.

3. Develop a personalized stress management program.

TIME REQUIRED

1 hour (30 minutes to complete the activity sheet and 30 minutes to discuss the activity in class)

PROCEDURE

1. Learners complete the activity sheet individually.

2. Following completion of the activity sheets, the instructor leads a class discussion on the responses to the activity.

3. The instructor may lead a more general class discussion based on the following questions.

DISCUSSION QUESTIONS

1. What are some of the physiological aspects of the stress response?

2. How do you balance or manage the demands of being a professional caregiver with the competing demands of being a parent, spouse, lover, or friend?

3. Why are women often expected to provide most of the informal caregiving in relationships? What effect does this have on women and on
   men?

4. What stress management practices have you found useful in coping
   with your own stressors?

Stress Management
for the Professional Caregiver

1. List five stressful situations that you experience as a professional caregiver or in your personal life. Describe your typical reactions to each situation.

2. For each of the above situations, list other responses that are available to you.

3. Develop guidelines for your own stress management plan. Your plan should cover the following areas:
   - Time management
   - Assertiveness
   - Nutrition
   - Relaxation
   - Exercise
   - Rest
   - Fun

PURPOSE

The purpose of this activity is to reveal to the learner the effect that over-involvement may have upon the behavior of the professional caregiver. Following the completion of this activity, the learner will be able to:

1. Discuss situations associated with stress when working with older people.

2. Develop strategies for effectively coping with feelings when dealing with older people.

TIME REQUIRED

45 minutes (25 minutes to complete the activity sheet and 20 minutes to discuss the activity in class)

PROCEDURE

1. The class is divided into pairs.

2. Each pair of students reads the case study and responds to the questions following the case.

3. Following completion of the activity sheets, the instructor leads a discussion of the activity.

4. The instructor may lead a more general discussion based on the following questions.

DISCUSSION QUESTIONS

1. Do you ever find your behavior affected by your feelings?

2. Are you able to respond to your clients' or family members' feelings?

3. What is the difference between attending to someone else's feelings and owning the feelings of another?

The Case of the Caring Professional

Read and analyze the following case and answer the questions that follow it.

June Robins, a health care worker, began working at a home health agency about 3 weeks ago. This is Ms. Robins' first job in which she will be working exclusively with older adults in a home setting.

During working hours, Ms. Robins thinks about her clients' feelings of loneliness. At the end of the workday, she has difficulty leaving her clients. She feels overwhelmed by anxiety and asks herself why she has these feelings.

During her off-duty hours, Ms. Robins begins to notice that she has intentionally filled her days with one activity after another. She realizes that her busy schedule prevents her from being alone.

While talking with a friend, Ms. Robins begins to verbalize some of her recent perceptions of her own behavior. Her friend asks her when she first became aware of this behavior and whether she thinks her behavior is connected with stress. Ms. Robins was not able to answer her friend. However, later that evening, she began to reflect on her work, her feelings, and the questions her friend had posed. After much thought, she began to recognize that she felt anxious about the loneliness that her older clients feel. She began to realize that she was transferring her clients' feelings to herself. This realization helped her review her options, which she identified as follows:

- Deny the feelings
- Avoid the feeling by seeking employment elsewhere
- Accept the feeling and identify it as anxiety associated with loneliness

1. Has Ms. Robins correctly identified her options?

2. What would you do if you were June Robins?

3. Think about your own experiences and professional situations. Share
    with your partner events and situations in which you have had diffi-
    culty separating your personal feelings and behaviors from your pro-
    fessional work.

4. How were you able to resolve these issues?

Appendix A

Evaluating the Effectiveness of Learning Activities

FOR THE EDUCATOR, A CRITICAL ASPECT OF THE EDUCATIONAL PROCESS IS THE evaluation of learning. Evaluation provides feedback to both the learner and the instructor on what learning has or has not taken place. In addition to pretests and posttests, which assess the level of knowledge, subjective evaluation of educational methods by the learner offers the educator an opportunity to evaluate attitudes and determine the benefits of a particular activity within the context of the learning environment. Evaluation aids in the preparation of presentations, as well as in determining modifications necessary to meet the needs of particular groups of learners. Soliciting learner input involves learners and encourages them to feel part of the learning process.

Learning Activity Evaluation Form

Please complete this evaluation form. Information received from your evaluation will assist in planning future learning activities. Your cooperation is appreciated.

Name of activity: _____

1. Do you feel that the learning activity increased your knowledge of older people and aging? (Circle your response.)

    Yes   No

2. How much time did it take you to complete the activity?

    ____ hours   ____ minutes

3. How well did this activity meet the stated objectives?

Excellent   Fair   Poor

  5   4   3   2   1
(All objectives   (None of the
were met.)   objectives
                                                        was met.)

4. Evaluate this activity as a learning experience.

Excellent   Fair   Poor

  5   4   3   2   1

5. Please make any additional comments regarding the learning activity.

Answer Key

The answer key contains answers to all of the quizzes and some of the learning activities contained in the book. Answers to the learning activities that require individual responses are not included.

Knowledge of Older Adults Quiz

1. **True** In 1989, adults 65 or older made up 12.5% of the population.

2. **True** By 2030, older adults will make up 22% of the total population.

3. **True** A relatively small number of babies were born during the Depression.

4. **True** A child born in 1988 could expect to live 74.9 years.

5. **False** Women 65 and over earned a median income of just over $5,000 in 1990.

6. **True** In 1988, arthritis was the most common chronic condition found in older Americans.

7. **False** In 1988, 9% of older adults had diabetes.

8. **False** According to 1990 data, 29% of older adults had hearing impairments.

9. **True** In 1989, there were 145 women over 65 for every 100 men over 65.

10. **True** In 1989, 77% of men over 65 and 42% of women over 65 were married.

11. **False** In 1989, the poverty rate for older women was 14%; the poverty rate for older men was 8%.

For answers to true/false items, see Fowles, D. (1990). *A profile of older Americans.* Washington, DC: American Association of Retired Persons and *Aging in the '80s.* (1990). Hyattsville, MD: Center for Health Statistics.

12. **True** In 1989, 49% of women over 65 were widows.

13. **True** In 1989, about one-third (31%) of African-Americans over 65 were poor.

14. **False** For the older population, the level of education has been steadily increasing. The median educational level of older adults increased from 8.7 years to 12.1 years between 1970 and 1988. In addition, the percentage of older adults who finished high school rose from 28% to 54%.

15. **True** A study conducted in 1984 found that 62% of older adults with children saw one of their offspring at least once a week.

Age Norming

Listed below are examples of socially prescribed obligations and privileges for each age group.

Age Group	Obligations	Privileges
20–29	Have a job or be in training or college; move away from parents' home	Legal rights as an adult (e.g., right to vote, right to drink)
30–39	Settle down with a mate and start a family	More responsibility at work
40–49	Provide financial support for children's education; if necessary, assist aging parents	Questioning of goals and accomplishments, which may lead to personal growth
50–59	Prepare for eventual retirement; maintain relationship with children and aging parents	"Empty nest," with its added freedom from pressures of child rearing
60–69	Finalize preparations for retirement; maintain relationship with adult children and grandchildren	Increased leisure time; release from pressures of a job
70 and older	Maintain one's independence for as long as possible; make adjustments based upon changes in health and finances	Increased leisure time; ability to become more active in church or community affairs

The Decade Game

Listed below are examples of significant historical events and values and behaviors for each decade from the 1930s through the 1980s.

Decade	Significant events	Promoted values and behavior
1930s	The Great Depression and massive unemployment	Having a job; being careful with money; saving for bad times
1940s	World War II; the atomic bombing of Hiroshima and Nagasaki	Patriotism regarding American involvement in the war; optimism
1950s	Korean War; start of school desegregation; McCarthy hearings; Sputnik, the Soviet satellite	Home ownership; family life as portrayed on television; working for only one employer for an entire career
1960s	Assassinations of President John F. Kennedy, Martin Luther King, and Robert Kennedy; war in Vietnam and protests against the war; urban riots	Racial equality; freedom to choose personal lifestyle; questioning of authority
1970s	End of war in Vietnam; Watergate; the oil embargo; start of the Iran hostage crisis	Self-oriented (the decade of "Me"); start of fitness craze; environmentalism
1980s	Reaganism, with its emphasis on deregulation and "trickle-down" economics; Irangate; the collapse of Communism in Eastern Europe; start of AIDS epidemic	Making money; "yuppies"; prevalence of the dual career family; gender equality; "safe" sex

The Aging Stereotype Game

Examples of negative stereotypes:

1. Older adults are lonely.

2. Older adults are frail.

3. Older adults are set in their ways.

4. Older adults are slow to learn.

5. Older adults are not productive.

6. Older adults are senile.

7. Older adults are hard of hearing.

8. Older adults have poor eyesight.

9. Older adults are sexless.

10. Older adults are wrinkled.

11. Older adults live in nursing homes.

12. Older adults fear death.

13. Older adults have little to do.

14. Older adults are depressed.

15. Older adults are poor.

16. Older adults are bald or have blue hair.

17. Older adults smell.

18. Older adults are bitter.

19. Older adults have bad attitudes about young people.

20. Older adults are bad drivers.

Examples of positive stereotypes:

1. Older adults are wise.

2. Older adults offer useful advice.

3. Older adults are rich.

4. Older adults are religious.

5. Older adults are politically active.

6. Older adults are good cooks.

7. Older adults are kind.

8. Older adults are more productive than younger persons.

9. Older adults are generous.

10. Older adults are good money managers.

11. Older adults work as volunteers.

12. Older adults love to travel.

13. Older adults love children.

14. Older adults have more freedom.

15. Older adults are well adjusted.

16. Older adults tell great stories.

17. Older adults are good listeners.

18. Older adults make friends easily.

19. Older adults are patient with family and friends.

20. Older adults are interesting.

Older Adults and Television

Name of show: Golden Girls

Type of show (comedy or drama): Comedy

There are four main characters in the series. Three are women between 54 and 65; one is a woman over 75.

One of the continuing characters is a daughter, another a mother. Several themes related to mother–daughter issues are addressed.

The entire program is devoted to themes on life and the process of aging. Themes related to retirement, changes in physical appearance, and sexuality are covered.

No conflicts between the generations were seen, with the exception of the conflicts between the mother and daughter, which appeared to be more family related than generational.

Knowledge of Physical Aging Quiz

1. **False** With age, the time period for the pulse rate to return to normal after exercise is lengthened (Cristofalo, 1988).

2. **True** As people age, their bones tend to lose calcium. This condition is known as osteoporosis (Fries, 1989).

3. **False** After the age of 70, approximately 1% of the neurons of the cortex are lost each year (Rybash, Roodin, & Santrock, 1991).

4. **False** Reaction time declines in middle and late adulthood (Rybash et al., 1991).

5. **True** Sagging and wrinkling reflect the loss of elasticity (Fries, 1989).

For answers to true/false items, see Cristofalo, V. (1988). An overview of the theories of biological aging. In J. Birren & V. Bengtson (Eds.), *Emergent theories of aging* (pp. 118–127). New York: Springer Publishing. Ferrini, A., & Ferrini, R. (1989). *Health in the later years*. Dubuque, IA: William C. Brown; Fowles, D. (1990). *A profile of older Americans*. Washington, DC: American Association of Retired Persons; Fries, J. (1989). *Aging well: A guide for successful seniors*. Reading, MA: Addison-Wesley; Rybash, J., Roodin, P., & Santrock, J. (1991). *Adult development and aging* (2nd ed.). Dubuque, IA: William C. Brown.

6. **True** Age spots are caused by cells producing too little or too much pigment (Fries, 1989).

7. **True** There are two general types of theories of physical aging: damage theories and programmed aging theories. Damage theories argue that human cells become damaged with age, causing the cells to function less efficiently. Programmed aging theories attribute bodily aging to an individual's genetic code (Ferrini & Ferrini, 1989).

8. **True** After age 45, most persons become more and more sensitive to glare (Rybash et al., 1991).

9. **True** Older adults seem to have more difficulty in processing speech sounds, but the cause of this deficit is unclear (Rybash et al., 1991).

10. **False** Over 80% of older adults have at least one chronic illness (Ferrini & Ferrini, 1989).

11. **True** There are large differences in the average life expectancies of various groups, with whites outliving African-Americans in the United States. Both of these groups outlive Hispanic-Americans (Ferrini & Ferrini, 1989).

12. **False** With age, our sensitivity to taste may decline. This decline appears to be less severe than the decline in hearing and vision (Rybash et al., 1991).

13. **True** Colorectal cancer among older Americans represent the second leading cause of death from cancer. The rate for people 75–79 is about four times that of people 55–59 (Ferrini & Ferrini, 1989).

14. **True** Nearly half of all older adults living outside long-term care facilities have arthritis (Fowles, 1990).

15. **True** With age, the arterial walls lose their elasticity. This results in a condition called arteriosclerosis (Ferrini & Ferrini, 1989).

Knowledge of Alzheimer's Disease Quiz

1. **True** Memory loss is an early manifestation of Alzheimer's disease. A decrease in learning speed and an increase in time for recall are part of the normal aging process. In Alzheimer's disease, however, forgetfulness involves daily activities to the degree that usual work-related tasks cannot be completed satisfactorily (Gwyther, 1985).

2. **True** Behavioral changes are important clues to the medical evaluation and appropriate management of the person with symptoms of dementia (Mace & Rabins, 1985).

3. **False** At this time, there is no medication that is effective in permanently delaying Alzheimer's disease. Unnecessary medication should be avoided (Greutzner, 1988).

4. **False** Alzheimer's disease is a degenerative process that results in atrophy that slowly progresses through the brain (Gwyther, 1985).

5. **True** Currently, no cause for Alzheimer's disease has been found. Research continues into several possible theories, including genetic and environmental factors and viruses. Alzheimer's disease is *not* caused by old age or hardening of the arteries (Gwyther, 1985).

6. **True** Tests are conducted to rule out other diseases that are associated with dementia. Only when these other causes for dementia have been ruled out is a diagnosis of Alzheimer's disease made. A definitive diagnosis can only be made by examination of brain tissue obtained on autopsy (Matteson & McConnell, 1988).

7. **True** Family members and caregivers frequently experience depression and grief during the time they are providing care to a person with Alzheimer's disease (Carroll, 1989).

8. **False** The progress of Alzheimer's disease is gradual, and most people with Alzheimer's disease live 10–12 years after diagnosis (Chenitz, Stone, & Salisbury, 1991).

9. **False** Alzheimer's disease is seen more frequently in women than in men. The reason for this is not known (Chenitz, Stone, & Salisbury, 1991).

10. **True** Depression is often experienced by the person with early Alzheimer's disease. Depression can also closely mimic the early signs of Alzheimer's disease (Carroll, 1989).

11. **False** There is great variability in the progression of Alzheimer's disease. Several phases have been identified, however. They include: early confusional phase, late confusional phase, early dementia, middle dementia, and late dementia (Matteson & McConnell, 1988).

12. **False** Alzheimer's disease causes a loss of intellectual and cognitive functioning, which leads to the inability to learn new mater-

For answers to true/false items, see Carroll, D. (1989). *When your loved one has Alzheimer's: A caregiver's guide.* New York: Harper & Row; Chenitz, W., Stone, J., & Salisbury, S. (1991). *Clinical gerontological nursing: A guide to advanced practice.* Philadelphia: W.B. Saunders; Greutzner, H. (1988). *Alzheimer's: A caregiver's guide and sourcebook.* New York: John Wiley & Sons; Gwyther, L.P. (1985). *Care of Alzheimer's patients: A manual for nursing home staff.* Washington, DC: American Health Care Association and Alzheimer's Association; Mace, N., & Rabins, P. (1985). *The 36-hour day. A family guide to caring for persons with Alzheimer's disease, related dementias, illnesses, and memory loss in later life.* Baltimore: Johns Hopkins University Press; and Matteson, M.M., & McConnell, E.S. (1988). *Gerontological nursing: Concepts and practice.* Philadelphia: W.B. Saunders.

ial. One way to assist a person with Alzheimer's disease is to provide a safe, secure, and familiar environment (Mace & Rabins, 1985).

13. **True** There is no cure for Alzheimer's disease. Research continues to investigate methods for treating the disease. Management measures are essential for the care and protection of the person with Alzheimer's disease (Matteson & McConnell, 1988).

14. **True** Support groups are very beneficial for caregivers of people with Alzheimer's disease. Such groups are made up of people who care for people with Alzheimer's disease (usually family members), and can be a source of support, information, and friendship. The Alzheimer's Association has chapters throughout the country. These chapters provide services, including support groups, for people with Alzheimer's disease and their families (Gwyther, 1985).

15. **True** Neurofibrillary tangles and senile plaques are two changes seen in the brains of people with Alzheimer's disease. These changes can be noted only after the death of the patient, through autopsy (Greutzner, 1988).

Knowledge of Sexuality and Aging Quiz

1. **True** Older men have more opportunities for sexual expression and more choice of female partners, because older women greatly outnumber them, and because they have a greater option to seek younger partners than is the case for older women. Apparently, it is more socially acceptable for men to have younger partners than for women. In addition, older men are much more likely to be married, while older women are more likely to be widowed (Turner & Helms, 1989).

2. **True** Sexual interest and activity in middle age appears to be related to continued activity later in life (Belsky, 1990).

3. **False** The level of responsiveness varies from person to person. To suggest that most older women are sexually unresponsive is to perpetuate an ageist myth. Many older women remain interested in sex, and a great many of those with available partners continue to be active sexually. Many older women as well as men view their sexual activity to be quite satisfactory (Butler et al., 1991).

4. **True** Diabetes mellitus, which is common in older adults, can cause impotence in older men. If the impotence is due to inadequate control of the diabetes, it may be corrected once control is reestablished. If impotence occurs in a diabetic male who has managed to maintain his diabetes, the impotence may be of a more permanent nature (Butler et al., 1991).

5. **True** For many older adults regular sexual activity may serve to reduce both psychological and physical tension. For example, sexual activity may benefit people with arthritis, because of the positive effect of cortisone, which is produced by the adrenal gland during physical activity (Butler et al., 1991).

6. **True** A self-fulfilling prophecy may develop, in which older people perceive themselves as unable to perform sexually and then become unable to do so. Cultural norms may also influence the expression of sexuality in older adults (Belsky, 1990; Ferrini & Ferrini, 1989).

7. **True** The pressure for older men to ejaculate is lessened because of a decreased volume of seminal fluid. Many women perceive this as a positive change because it extends the period of erection. Older men may not perceive the need to ejaculate as quickly (Turner & Helms, 1989).

8. **True** As women age, the amount of lubricant decreases and the vaginal wall gradually becomes less elastic (Turner & Helms, 1989).

9. **True** Generally, older adults require more time for precoital stimulation (Turner & Helms, 1989).

10. **True** Prostate dysfunction may affect sexual responsiveness. About half of all men over age 80 have prostate dysfunction (Turner & Helms, 1989).

11. **False** The vast majority of older adults are not fragile, and their health is not endangered by sexual intercourse (Butler & Lewis, 1981).

12. **True** In 1989, there were 145 women 65 and over for every 100 older men. Seventy-seven percent of older men were married, compared to 42 percent of older women (Fowles, 1990).

13. **True** Male masturbation helps to preserve erectile ability; female masturbation helps maintain the elasticity and lubrication of the vagina (Butler et al., 1991).

14. **True** One inhibiting factor for older adults living in long-term care facilities appears to be privacy. This lack of privacy may exist for married as well as unmarried residents (Ferrini & Ferrini, 1989).

15. **True** Men who are unable physically to produce an erection can receive a surgically inserted device, which will allow them to achieve an erection (Butler et al., 1991).

For answers to true/false items, see Belsky, J. (1990). *The psychology of aging: Theory, research, and interventions* (2nd ed.). Pacific Grove, CA: Brooks/Cole; Butler, R., Lewis, M., & Sunderland, T. (1991). *Aging and mental health: Positive psychosocial and biomedical approaches* (4th ed.). New York: MacMillan; Ferrini, A., & Ferrini, R. (1989). *Health in the later years.* Dubuque, IA: William C. Brown; Fowles, D. (1990). *A profile of older Americans.* Washington, DC: American Association of Retired Persons; Turner, J., & Helms, D. (1989). *Contemporary adulthood* (4th ed.). Fort Worth, TX: Holt, Rinehart, & Winston.

Applying the Resident's Bill of Rights

1. The rights to privacy, to share a room with a spouse, and to visitor access are being violated. The appropriate action would be to knock before entering a resident's room and to provide time for spouses to be together privately.

2. The right to be informed about one's care and medical treatment and the right to participate in the medical care provided are being violated. The appropriate action would be to inform the resident about the medication, to explain why the physician ordered it, to discuss the side effects of the medication, and to encourage the resident to call her doctor if she has further questions.

3. The right to manage one's financial affairs is being violated. A quarterly accounting of all monies held by the facility must be made. The appropriate action would be to obtain a copy of the financial records and allow the resident to review them. The staff should answer any questions the resident may have about how the money is used.

4. The right to voice grievances is being violated. The appropriate action would be to give the resident a copy of the facility's grievance procedure and let him voice his complaints to a staff member. The name and phone number of the local ombudsman should be posted in a prominent place in the facility.

5. The right to considerate and respectful care is being violated. The appropriate action would be to avoid discussing resident care in public places.

6. The right to privacy and the right to dignity are being violated. The appropriate action would be to pull the curtain around the bed when bathing a resident and to close the door to the room prior to providing daily personal care and hygiene.

7. The right to be informed of the rights, rules, and regulations governing resident conduct and responsibility is being violated. The appropriate action would be to provide each resident with a copy of the resident's rights and responsibilities, and the regulations of the facility at the time of admission.

8. The right to choose one's physician is being violated. The appropriate action would be to ask the resident if he had a particular physician he preferred to treat him in the nursing home. The resident's choice should be honored and orders for medical care and treatment should be obtained from the resident's physician.

9. The right to self-administer medications, if determined safe by the professionals caring for the resident, is being violated. The appropri-

ate action would be to determine from the physician if the resident can safely self-administer medication. If the physician approves self-administration and the resident prefers to self-administer medication, the staff should allow the resident to do so.

10. The right to privacy is being violated. The appropriate action would be to provide a room where the resident and spouse can visit with each other and/or engage in sexual activity in private.

11. The right to access to and private use of a telephone is being violated. The appropriate action would be to allow residents regular access to a private area for telephone conversations.

12. The right to choose activities, schedules, and healthcare consistent with one's own interests and plan for care is being violated. The appropriate action would be to ask the resident's preference in scheduling activities for the day, including bath time, meals, meetings, and therapy. Staff should try to accommodate the resident's preferences.

13. The right to have personal possessions, as space permits, is being violated. The appropriate action would be to allow the resident to use his/her belongings as chosen.

14. The right to send and receive mail is being violated. The appropriate action would be to deliver all mail to the resident as it is received by the facility.

15. The right to be free from physical restraint is being violated. The appropriate action would be to untie the resident unless the resident's safety is at stake.

Welcome to Our Nursing Home: Facilitating Adjustment

1. Mr. Johnson's family might have considered an assisted living arrangement, under which Mr. Johnson would continue to live independently, but would receive help in some of his activities of daily living.

2a. Mr. Johnson's family should consider the following in selecting a nursing home:

Is the nursing home clean? Is there an odor in the facility?

What are the residents' rooms like? Are the rooms big enough to accommodate personal items?

Where are the bathrooms located? Are bathrooms and bathing areas equipped with grab bars?

Do the nurses appear to respond promptly to residents' requests?

Is the food appealing?

Is there an activity room for the residents? Are a variety of activities offered?

Is physical therapy available? How often is it provided?

Is a physician available in case of emergency?

Are the staff cheerful and courteous?

Are residents dressed and out of their rooms?

Is the Resident's Bill of Rights prominently displayed?

What are the facility's visiting hours?

What have other people said about the facility? Does it have a good reputation in the community?

b.   Before Mr. Johnson moves to the facility, arrangements must be made with the nursing home regarding how the services will be paid for; medical records will need to be sent to the nursing home; personal articles and clothing will need to be brought from home; and transportation will need to be arranged to move Mr. Johnson to the facility.

Annotated Bibliography

Introduction: Teaching Activities for the Study of Gerontology

Bonwell, C., & Eison, J. (1991). *Active learning creating excitement in the classroom*. ASHE-ERIC Higher Report *91*(1). Washington, DC: Eric Clearinghouse in Higher Education.

This report encourages teachers to include experiential learning in their courses. Teachers may use active learning techniques without dramatically changing their teaching styles.

Brazil, M.J. (1990). *Building library collections on aging: A selection guide and rare list*. Santa Barbara, CA: ABC-Clio.

This resource is a guide to obtaining information on aging issues. Included are lists of publishers, prices of materials, and ways of acquiring all titles. A number of government documents are listed, as well as free or inexpensive materials.

Chene, A. (1991). Self-esteem of the elderly and education. *Educational Gerontology, 17,* 343–353.

In this well-written article, the author clarifies issues related to self-esteem, self-concept, and loss as they affect adult learning and education.

Johnson, D., & Johnson, F. (1987). *Joining together: Group theory and group skills* (3rd ed.). Englewood Cliffs, NJ: Prentice Hall.

This book is an excellent example of merging content with practical learning experiences. For every major topic in the field of group dynamics, the authors have included structured classroom activities.

Sinnott, J., et al. (1983). *Applied research in aging: A guide to methods and research*. Boston: Little, Brown.

This book offers a comprehensive and practical guide to applied gerontological research. The authors describe sampling, measurement tools, and resources for research. An appendix on bibliographic sources, clearinghouses, and funding is included.

White, R. (1989). Fostering insight into personal conceptions of the elderly: A simulation exercise. *Teaching of Psychology, 16*(4), 216–218.

In this article, a class exercise in which students play the role of older adults is described. Learners simulate both the appearance and physical constraints facing many older people.

Chapter 1: Perceptions of Aging

Atchley, R. (1985). *Social forces and aging: An introduction to social gerontology* (4th ed.). Belmont, CA: Wadsworth.

This book provides a thorough survey of social gerontology. The treatments of humor and aging, attitudes about aging, and television and aging are particularly useful.

Cowgill, D. (1986). *Aging around the world.* Belmont, CA: Wadsworth.

This book on cross-cultural aspects of aging includes a thorough examination of the author's theory of modernization. Included are chapters on value systems and aging, kinship, and the effects of economic systems on the status of older adults.

Cozby, P. (1989). *Methods in behavioral research* (4th ed.). Mountain View, CA: Mayfield.

This book shows how the scientific method is applied to behavioral research. Included are thorough treatments of ethical concerns, experimental design, and the mechanics of writing research reports.

Fowles, D. (1990). *A profile of older Americans.* Washington, DC: American Association of Retired Persons.

This pamphlet contains information about the older population in the United States. It is updated annually with the most recent statistics on people over 65.

Fowles, D. (1987). The numbers game. *Aging, 356,* 44–45.

The author derides those who cite incorrect statistics about older adults. In this easy-to-read article, Fowles makes projections about the number of older adults in the United States in the future.

Holden, C. (1987). Why do women live longer than men? *Science, 238,* 158–160.

Holden describes the state of the art thinking on why women live longer than men, and concludes that the explanation remains elusive.

Skinner, B.F., & Vaughan, M.E. (1983). *Enjoy old age: A program of self-management.* New York: Norton.

Coauthored by the late behaviorist, B.F. Skinner, and M.E. Vaughan, a gerontologist, this book offers practical tips for older persons on issues ranging from memory and sensory enhancement to freedom and dignity. Written as a self-help guide, the book is published in large print.

Swisher, K. (Ed.). (1990). *The elderly: Opposing viewpoints.* San Diego: Greenhaven Press.

Through the use of popular readings and several activities, the book examines the development of critical thinking skills. Social science faculty may find this book a useful addition to an undergraduate course on aging.

Chapter 2: Stereotyping and Ageism

Age Ware, Inc. (1988). *New images of aging* (video, ¹/₂" VHS, 30 minutes). Emeryville, CA.

This videotape examines current trends of an aging population, focusing on customs and popular beliefs about aging. Misconceptions are corrected by the presentation of facts and certain beliefs are debunked as myths.

Arluke, A., & Levin, J. (1984). Another stereotype: Old age as a second childhood. *Aging, 346,* 7–11.

The authors describe infantilization as an especially damaging ageist stereotype. They argue that infantilization of older adults is widespread and that this conception reinforces gerontophobia, a neurotic fear of becoming old.

Atchley, R. (1985). *Social forces and aging: An introduction to social gerontology* (4th ed.). Belmont, CA: Wadsworth.

This book provides a thorough survey of social gerontology. The treatments of humor and aging, attitudes about aging, and television and aging are useful.

Barrow, G. (1989). *Aging, the individual, and society* (4th ed.). St. Paul: West.

The text is a highly readable introduction to social gerontology. Especially helpful is the material found in the second chapter, "Stereotypes and Images."

Binstock, R. (1983). The aged as scapegoat. *The Gerontologist, 23,* 136–143.

Binstock argues that our perceptions of older adults have changed in that we now see them as affluent and politically powerful. This article is valuable reading on the politics of aging.

Buchholz, M., & Byrum, J. (1982). Newspaper presentation of America's aged: A content analysis of image and role. *The Gerontologist, 22,* 83–88.

Buchholz and Byrum examined coverage of older adults in two daily newspapers, the *Daily Oklahoman* and the *New York Times.* Although coverage of older people was generally positive, both papers failed to inform readers adequately about pertinent social policy issues affecting older people.

Butler, R. (1975). *Why survive? Being old in America.* New York: Harper & Row.

This Pulitzer Prize—winning book documents what the author, an eminent gerontologist, saw as the tragedy of older adulthood in America. Butler coined the term *ageism,* and is also credited with awakening the American public to the plight of older people.

Covey, H. (1988). Historical terminology used to represent older people. *The Gerontologist, 28,* 291–297.

Using the *Oxford English Dictionary* and other sources, Covey traces the development of English terms for older adults. He finds differences in the types of terms applied to men and women and notes the very negative nature of most of the terms, a trend that appears to have worsened since about 1875.

Demos, V., & Jacha, A. (1981). When you care enough: An analysis of attitudes toward aging in humorous birthday cards. *Gerontologist, 21,* 209–215.

This interesting study demonstrates the merging of sexism with ageism in birthday cards. The article is appropriate for both faculty and students.

Dillon, K., & Jones, B. (1981). Attitudes toward aging portrayed by birthday cards. *International Journal of Aging and Human Development, 13,* 79–84.

This article reports the results of a study using content analysis to evaluate attitudes toward aging as depicted in birthday cards. Six thematic categories—loss, age concealment, sympathy or respect for elders, not showing one's age, things getting better with age, and age as a matter of mind—were identified. Overall attitudes were found to be negative.

Esposito, J. (1987). *The obsolete self: Philosophical dimensions of aging.* Berkeley: University of California Press.

Esposito examines a number of important philosophical issues confronting aging and analyzes ageism, paternalism, and social justice, stressing practical, clinical, and social concerns. The book is appropriate for faculty in the health sciences, social sciences, and humanities.

Huyck, J.M., & Duchon, J. (1986). Over the miles: Coping, communicating and commiserating through age-theme greeting cards. In L. Nahemow, K. McClusky-Fawcett, & P. McGee (Eds.), *Humor and aging* (pp. 139–159). Orlando, FL: Academic Press.

This chapter describes the authors' findings on the use of greeting cards as a method for coping with anxieties over aging. These researchers analyzed the meaning of sending selected cards.

Jeffreys-Fox, B. (1977). *How realistic are television's portrayals of the elderly?* Baltimore: University Park Press.

Jeffreys-Fox found the majority (75 percent) of older characters in television shows to be men. Older characters were evaluated more negatively than younger characters in terms of warmth, attractiveness, and intelligence.

Nuessel, F. (1982). The language of ageism. *The Gerontologist, 22,* 273–276.

Nuessel wonders just how we might refer to people who are 65 years of age or older. He suggests the use of "elderly" since it appears to be neutral and devoid of ageist connotation. This paper makes a convincing case for the importance of carefully choosing words, since stereotypic terms reflect social myths.

Nussbaum, J., Thompson, T., & Robinson, J. (1989). *Communication and aging.* New York: Harper & Row.

This book provides a thorough treatment of communication and older adults. Among the stronger chapters are those covering attitudes and ageism, relational considerations, and the mass media. A section on age-related barriers in conversation may be very useful to practitioners.

Palmore, E. (1986). Attitudes toward aging shown by humor: A review. In L. Nahemow, K. McClusky-Fawcett, & P. McGee (Eds.), *Humor and Aging* (pp. 101–119). Orlando, FL: Academic Press.

Palmore provides the most comprehensive view of humor and attitudes about aging that we have found. The author surveys research about jokes, cartoons, and birthday cards, and makes insightful suggestions concerning future research.

Penrod, S. (1986). *Social psychology* (2nd ed.). Englewood Cliffs, NJ: Prentice Hall.

Penrod presents a thorough treatment of the social psychology of stereotypes. He includes a special section on ageist stereotypes.

Peterson, M. (1973). The visibility and image of old people on television. *Journalism Quarterly, 50,* 569–573.

Using content analysis, Peterson found that about 60 percent of the older characters were depicted favorably. A useful paper for students and faculty.

Chapter 3: Physical Aging

Carroll, D. (1989). *When your loved one has Alzheimer's: A caregiver's guide.* New York: Harper & Row.

Written for the family caregiver, this book offers concrete advice and strategies for dealing effectively with a family member with Alzheimer's disease. Especially helpful are the chapters on "Alzheimering" the home, on the caregiver's coping with personal emotional needs, and on obtaining help. This book is an excellent resource for community health educators.

Chenitz, W., Stone, J., & Salisbury, S. (1991). *Clinical gerontological nursing: A guide to advanced practice.* Philadelphia: W.B. Saunders.

As an advanced clinical gerontological text, this book is designed to be used as a reference to foster new ideas and creativity in the clinical and administrative environment. The contributors to this book are practicing clinicians, researchers and educators.

Crewe, N. (1990). Aging and severe physical disability: Patterns and implications for services. *Educational Gerontology, 16*(6), 525–534.

Normal physical changes of aging have affected individuals with disabilities and have precipitated new needs for services. Professionals are challenged to address the issues of wellness, not just disability, and develop services that enable independence.

Cristofalo, V. (1988). An overview of the theories of biological aging. In J. Birren & V. Bengtsm (Eds.), *Emergent theories of aging* (pp. 118–127). New York: Springer Publishing.

The author describes some of the basic physical processes of aging and briefly summarizes several biological theories. This chapter should prove helpful to both faculty and students. Readers seeking technical references will find the sources cited by Cristofalo useful.

Ferrini, A., & Ferrini, R. (1989). *Health in the later years.* Dubuque, IA: William C. Brown.

This text is a highly readable survey of health issues affecting older adults. It contains an excellent summary of demographic data. Chapters on chronic illness, medication use, and sexuality are presented effectively.

Fries, J. (1989). *Aging well: A guide for successful seniors.* Reading, MA: Addison-Wesley.

This highly readable book includes a wealth of easy-to-read information on a wide range of health care topics. It should prove useful to older adults, caregivers, students, and educators.

Gruetzner, H. (1988). *Alzheimer's: A caregiver's guide and sourcebook.* New York: John Wiley & Sons.

Designed for use by family caregivers, this book includes material on symptoms and phases of Alzheimer's disease, possible causes of the disease, the relationship between Alzheimer's disease and depression, common myths about the disease, and strategies for coping and adjusting. The book is an excellent resource for family and professional caregivers as well as educators.

Gwyther, Lisa P. (1985). *Care of Alzheimer's patients: A manual for nursing home staff.* Washington, DC: American Health Care Association and Alzheimer's Association.

This book was written primarily for nursing home staff and contains practical information about the daily care needs of people with

Alzheimer's disease. In addition to factual information about the disease, the book describes cases that nursing home staff might encounter in their work, and cites solutions to dealing with the problems presented.

Higginbotham, J. (1991). The Americans with Disabilities Act. *FBI Law Enforcement Bulletin, 60,* 25–32.

The author provides details concerning the law that was signed by the President in July of 1990. Health care educators and administrators can gain much from this article.

Lee, V. (1991). Language changes and Alzheimer's disease: A literature review. *Journal of Gerontological Nursing, 17,* 16–20.

Lee provides an excellent review of cognitive changes associated with Alzheimer's disease. Included is a section covering implications for nursing practice.

Mace, N., & Rabins, P. (1985). *The 36-hour day. A family guide to caring for persons with Alzheimer's disease, related dementias, illnesses, and memory loss in later life.* Baltimore: Johns Hopkins University Press.

This book, written for the caregiver, offers practical suggestions for dealing with all aspects of Alzheimer's disease. It is a classic in the field. It is well-written, easy to read, and pragmatic in its approach.

Matteson, M.A., & McConnell, E.S. (1988). *Gerontological nursing: Concepts and practice.* Philadelphia: W.B. Saunders.

This comprehensive book on gerontological nursing provides an overview of the field. Topics covered include a conceptual framework for gerontologic practice, age-related changes, psychosocial considerations, and clinical issues. Numerous tables, diagrams and figures illustrate the concepts and principles discussed throughout the book. This text could be used as a primary sourcebook for nurses and other professionals who care for older people in a variety of health care settings.

Media Creations Corporation. (1985). *Aging: A positive experience of growth* (four video tapes, $1/2$" VHS, 30 minutes). Cleveland, OH.

In this series of videotapes, older people are motivated to be responsible for their own health. Each videotape can be used alone. The four titles are: *Physical changes of age, Psychosocial aspects of aging, Maintaining independence,* and *Aging: Living life fully.*

National Research Council. (1989). *Diet and health.* Washington, DC: National Academy Press.

This book contains reports and recommendations of dietary requirements for improving health and reducing the risks of chronic disease. The most current research has been examined by experts in the field and is described in detail.

Oliver, R., & Bock, F. (1987). *Coping with Alzheimer's: A caregiver's emotional survival guide.* New York: Dodd, Mead, and Company.

The authors describe how rational emotive therapy (RET), a form of cognitive restructuring, can be used to help caregivers deal with the psychological issues that often accompany coping with the dementia of a friend or family member.

Rybash, J., Roodin, P., & Santrock, J. (1991). *Adult development and aging* (2nd ed.). Dubuque, IA: William C. Brown.

This book can be used as a textbook in adult development or the psychology of aging. Among the strongest chapters are those on the nature of development, the biological processes affecting aging, and cognition.

Scott, R., Bramble, K., & Goodyear, N. (1991). How knowledge and labeling of dementia affect nurses' expectations. *Journal of Gerontological Nursing, 17,* 21–24.

Nursing staff were shown to possess considerable knowledge of dementia. In-service educators may be able to use the 10-item knowledge questionnaire.

Thornton, H. (1989). *A medical handbook for senior citizens and their families.* Dover, MA: Auburn House.

Patient. education specialists could benefit from this practical book, which includes useful sections on high blood pressure, osteoporosis, diabetes, falls and mobility problems, and problems with feet.

Verbrugge, L. (1990). The iceberg of disability. In S. Stahl (Ed.), *The legacy of longevity: Health and health care in later life* (pp. 55–75). Newbury Park, CA: Sage Publications.

This volume takes a social science perspective in looking at chronic disease and disability.

Video Press, University of Maryland. (1987). *What is dementia?* (video, 1/2" VHS, 16 minutes). Baltimore, MD.

This videotape defines dementia and examines its causes. Alzheimer's disease is distinguished from other forms of dementia. There is a positive focus on the older person's strengths, on providing emotional support, and on treating the older person's physical symptoms.

Chapter 4: Psychological Aging

Aldwin, C., Spiro, A., Bosse, R., & Levenson, M. (1989). Longitudinal findings from the normative aging study: 1. Does mental health change with age? *Psychology and Aging, 3,* 295–306.

Examining over 2,000 middle-aged and older adults, Aldwin et al. found no link between age and psychological distress. The article should prove interesting to faculty and students in psychology and other related fields.

Atchley, R. (1985). *Social forces and aging: An introduction to social gerontology* (4th ed.). Belmont, CA: Wadsworth.

This book provides a thorough survey of social gerontology. The treatments of humor and aging, attitudes about aging, and television and aging are particularly useful.

Atkinson, R.M. (1988). Alcoholism in the elderly population. *Mayo Clinic Proceedings*, 63, 825–828.

This editorial serves as a summary of some of the significant research findings on alcoholism among older adults. Although the material covered is technical in nature, the author's style is clear, making the article less difficult to understand than many papers appearing in medical journals. This paper should prove highly useful to both health care providers and faculty.

Baltes, P., Reese, W., & Lipsitt, L. (1980). Lifespan development psychology. *Annual Review of Psychology, 31,* 65–110.

The authors provide a thorough treatment of the normative and nonnormative effects on adult development. This article is suitable for students and faculty in the social sciences.

Belsky, J. (1990). *The psychology of aging: Theory, research, and interventions* (2nd ed.). Pacific Grove, CA: Brooks/Cole.

This text provides a good overview of the psychology of aging. Especially strong are the sections on sexuality and depression in later life.

Billig, N. (1987). *To be old and sad: Understanding depression in the elderly.* Lexington, MA: Lexington Books.

This superbly written book offers useful information for older persons as well as caregivers. Billig, a psychiatrist, avoids "pop" psychological quick-fixes and guides the reader through symptomology, treatment, pharmacology, and the differences between depression and other illnesses.

Birren, J., & Schaie, K. (Eds.). (1990). *Handbook of the psychology of aging* (3rd ed.). San Diego: Academic Press.

Psychology and nursing faculty should find this a rich source of information on a wide range of topics. Especially thought provoking are the chapters on creativity and caregiving.

Bonner, J., & Harris, W. (1988). *Healthy aging: New directions in health, biology and medicine.* Claremont, CA: Hunter House.

An outgrowth of an extension course on the biology of aging, this book is a readable guide for educators, older people, and caregivers. Complex physiological processes are simplified in chapters ranging from diet to the immune system.

Borgatta, E., Montgomery, R., & Borgatta, M. (1982). Alcohol use and abuse: Life crisis events and the elderly. *Research on Aging, 4,* 378–408.

This paper outlines some of the inconsistencies in the literature on alcohol and older adults. It coincides with a request for better designed studies on the subject. The somewhat technical paper is appropriate for faculty and graduate students in the health and social sciences.

Butler, R., Lewis, M., & Sunderland, T. (1991). *Aging and mental health: Positive psychosocial and biomedical approaches* (4th ed.). New York: Macmillan.

This text contains comprehensive sections on successful aging, psychiatric disorders, organic mental disorders, keeping older adults in the home, and appropriate institutional care. Included are valuable appendices describing sources of literature on geriatrics and gerontology, training and educational material, and a historical summary of U.S. policies on aging.

Costa, P., & McCrae, R. (1984). Concurrent validation after 20 years: The implications of personality stability for its assessment. In N. Shock, R. Greulich, R. Andres, D. Arenberg, P. Costa, E. Lakatta, & J. Tobin (Eds.), *Normal human aging: The Baltimore longitudinal study of aging* (NIH Publication No. 84-2450). Washington, DC: U.S. Public Health Service.

This article provides a summary of Costa's research on stability in personality. It is most appropriate for faculty and graduate students in the social and health sciences.

Finlayson, R., Hurt, R., Davis, L., & Morse, R. (1988). Alcoholism in elderly persons: A study of the psychiatric and psychosocial features of 216 inpatients. *Mayo Clinic Proceedings, 63,* 761–768.

This article examines the medical records of 216 older adults admitted to the Alcohol and Drug Dependence Unit of the Mayo Clinic and Rochester Methodist Hospital. The research found that additional psychological disorders were common in the patient population. This is a technical report that should prove valuable to mental health faculty and practitioners.

Maas, H., & Kuypers, J. (1974). *From thirty to seventy: A forty-year study of adult life styles and personality.* San Francisco: Jossey-Bass.

Maas and Kuypers examined the adult life course of 142 persons. This well-written book is recommended for faculty and graduate students.

McAdams, D. (1990). *The person: An introduction to personality psychology.* San Diego: Harcourt Brace Jovanovich.

This text offers a holistic and biographical view of personality. The theme of the book is clearly reflected in such chapters as "Identity and the Life Story" and "The Biography of the Adult." The author makes frequent references to literature and mythology.

Shneidman, E. (1989). The Indian summer of life: A preliminary study of septuagenarians. *American Psychologist, 44,* 684–694.

The author analyzes changes in 11 septuagenarians. All of the subjects were male lawyers who were evaluated in terms of dimensions of life satisfaction. Shneidman perceives the seventh decade of life as an Indian Summer. His paper makes for interesting reading.

Stall, R. (1986). Change and stability in quantity and frequency of alcohol use among aging males: A 19-year follow-up study. *British Journal of Addiction, 81,* 537–544.

The author conducted interviews with a sample of people who had been interviewed in 1964. The study revealed little change in the frequency of drinking. Those subjects who did change their patterns of consumption were almost twice as likely to have decreased their level of drinking than they were to have increased it. This technical paper is recommended for faculty and students with an interest in alcohol use by older adults.

Chapter 5: Sexuality and Aging

Belsky, J. (1990). *The psychology of aging: Theory, research, and interventions* (2nd ed.). Pacific Grove, CA: Brooks/Cole.

This text provides a good overview of psychological topics in aging. Especially strong are the sections on sexuality and depression in later life.

Ferrini, A., & Ferrini, R. (1989). *Health in the later years.* Dubuque, IA: William C. Brown.

This text is a highly readable survey of health issues affecting older adults. It contains an excellent summary of demographic data. Chapters on chronic illness, medication use, and sexuality are presented effectively.

Lichtenberg, P., & Strzepek, D. (1990). Assessments of institutionalized dementia patients' competencies to participate in intimate relationships. *The Gerontologist, 30,* 117–120.

This practical article provides guidelines to help nursing home staff determine competency for sexual relationships. It may cause the reader to reexamine personal attitudes about sexuality and older adults.

Litz, B., Zeiss, A., & Davies, H. (1990). Sexual concerns of male spouses of female Alzheimer's disease patients. *The Gerontologist, 30,* 113–116.

This article examines the case of a 72-year-old male caregiver whose spouse has been diagnosed as having Alzheimer's disease. The sexual needs and feelings of guilt of the caregiver are examined. Important implications for clinical practice make this article valuable for professional caregivers.

Masters, W., & Johnson, V. (1966). *Human sexual response.* Boston: Little, Brown.

This groundbreaking book provides a wealth of data on human sexuality. It is recomended for faculty and advanced students in the health sciences.

McCartney, J., Izeman, H., Rogers, D., & Cohen, N. (1987). Sexuality and the institutionalized elderly. *Journal of the American Geriatrics Society, 35,* 331–333.

This article includes two case histories of nursing home residents. The authors conclude that nursing home staff should try to be supportive of the sexual needs of nursing home residents.

Turner, J., & Helms, D. (1989). *Contemporary adulthood* (4th ed.). Fort Worth, TX: Holt, Rinehart, & Winston.

This text on adult development contains outstanding chapters on retirement, bereavement, and grief. A brief section on sexuality should prove useful to educators.

Chapter 6: Family Issues in Aging

Atchley, R. (1985). *Social forces and aging: An introduction to social gerontology* (4th ed.). Belmont, CA: Wadsworth.

This book provides a thorough survey of social gerontology. The treatments of humor and aging, attitudes about aging, and television and aging are useful.

Barrow, G. (1989). *Aging, the individual, and society* (4th ed.). St. Paul, MN: West.

This textbook includes useful information on demographics, ageist stereotypes, theories of aging, and family issues. The book is both comprehensive and readable.

Brody, E. (1985). Parent care as a normative family stress. *The Gerontologist, 25,* 19–29.

Millions of Americans, mostly women, care for frail older family members. Brody views many of these adult children as caught between the competing demands of their older parents, their spouses and children, and their jobs. This article is important reading for educators and professionals working with older adults.

Butler, R. (1975) *Why survive? Being old in America.* New York: Harper & Row.

Cicirelli, V. (1983). Adult children and their parents. In T. Brubaker (Ed.), *Family relationships in later life* (pp. 31–46). Beverly Hills, CA: Sage Publications.

The author uses attachment theory to explain the give and take that occurs between adult children and their parents. This theory may help to explain why the majority of adults have good relationships with their parents.

Cicirelli, V. (1985). Sibling relationships throughout the life cycle. In L. L'Abate (Ed.), *The handbook of family psychology and therapy, vol. I* (pp. 177–214). Homewood, IL: Dorsey Press.

This chapter offers a comprehensive review of the scientific literature regarding siblings throughout the life span. The material is difficult and the chapter is thus recommended for advanced undergraduate and graduate students and college faculty only.

Doka, K., & Mertz, M. (1988). The meaning and significance of great-grandparenthood. *The Gerontologist, 28,* 192–197.

Doka and Mertz interviewed 40 great-grandparents and identified two distinct styles of grandparenting, remote and close. Students and faculty in the social sciences should find this article valuable.

Heinemann, G. (1983). Family involvement and support for widowed persons. In T. Brubaker (Ed.), *Family relationships in later life* (pp. 127–148). Beverly Hills, CA: Sage Publications.

This article is a highly readable essay on kin involvement with the widowed. Especially interesting are the sections on sources of strain in family relationships, renegotiation of roles with children, continued ties to the deceased spouse, and the family as support system.

Herr, J., & Weakland, J. (1979). *Counseling elders and their families: Practical techniques for applied gerontology.* New York: Springer Publishing Company.

Written from a family systems perspective, this text provides practical information and techniques for people who counsel older adults and their families. The chapter on family problem solving and interwoven case material are especially useful.

Hickey, T., & Douglass, R. (1981). Neglect and abuse of older family members: Professional perspectives and case experiences. *The Gerontologist, 21,* 171–176.

This article examines the experiences of 228 service providers who were interviewed regarding neglect and abuse of older adults by family members. To explain the causes of abuse, the authors developed a life-cycle model. The article is useful for educators and service providers.

Kosberg, J. (1985). Assistance to crime and abuse victims. In A. Monk (Ed.), *Handbook of gerontological services* (pp. 365–382). New York: Van Nostrand.

Kosberg reviews six theoretical explanations of elder abuse:

1) psychopathology, 2) sociological, 3) social exchange, 4) life crisis, 5) social-structural, and 6) intergenerational. This paper is appropriate for faculty and graduate students.

Maddox, G. (1991). Who cares? *The Gerontologist, 31,* 275–277.

Maddox reviews four books involving caring relationships. The books concern women and caregiving, foster families, a professional's guide for helping aging families, and a British text on the caring relationship. Maddox has very high praise for Elaine Brody's *Women in the middle: Their parent-care years.*

Matthews, S., & Sprey, J. (1984). The impact of divorce on grandparenthood: An exploratory study. *The Gerontologist, 24,* 41–47.

This study examines how grandparents are affected when their adult children get divorced. It should prove useful to educators and professionals working with older adults.

O'Bryant, S., & Morgan, L. (1990). Recent widows' kin support and orientations to self-sufficiency. *The Gerontologist, 30,* 391–398.

Findings of this study suggest that many widows are self-sufficient, but rely mainly on their adult children when they need assistance.

Quinn, M., & Tomita, S. (1986). *Elder abuse and neglect: Causes, diagnosis, and intervention strategies.* New York: Springer Publishing.

This book presents a thorough account of the prevalence, causes, assessment, and treatment of abuse and neglect. Educators and professionals working with older adults should find this text useful.

Troll, L. (1983). Grandparents: The family watchdogs. In T. Brubaker (Ed.), *Family relationships in later life* (pp. 63–74). Beverly Hills, CA: Sage Publications.

The author shows that many grandparents help their children and grandchildren when the need arises. The chapter is appropriate for faculty and advanced students in the social sciences.

Chapter 7: Maximizing Choices

Achenbaum, A. (1983). *Shades of grey: Old age, American values, and federal policies since 1920.* Boston: Little, Brown.

Achenbaum provides an interesting history of U.S. policies toward older adults. Faculty in the social sciences, especially those in sociology, history, and political science, will gain much from this volume.

Atchley, R. (1985). *Social forces and aging: An introduction to social gerontology* (4th ed.). Belmont, CA: Wadsworth.

Atchley's book is one of the most thoroughly researched of all the available general texts in social gerontology. Since much of Atchley's own research covers the topic of retirement, the chapter on retirement is particularly strong. While this text is thorough, it is not as readable as several other available general texts.

Barrow, G. (1989). *Aging, the individual and society* (4th ed.). St. Paul, MN: West Publishing.

This text includes useful information on family issues and finances. The book is both comprehensive and readable.

Cockerham, W. (1991). *The aging society.* Englewood Cliffs, NJ: Prentice-Hall.

This well-researched book makes an excellent text for a course in social gerontology. Faculty and students will benefit from the sections on work, retirement, and social policy.

Cutler, N., & Gregg, D. (1991). The human "wealth span" and financial well-being in older age. *Generations, 15,* 45–48.

Cutler and Gregg analyze the meaning of financial security and introduce the concept of "wealth span." This highly readable article should prove useful to educators and students in the social sciences.

Easterlin, R., Macdonald, C., & Macunovich, D. (1990). Retirement prospects of the baby boom generation: A different perspective. *The Gerontologist, 30,* 776–783.

The authors contend that baby boomers are more likely than members of earlier cohorts to begin old age in a solid financial position. This fascinating paper is appropriate for faculty in the social sciences.

Lubomudrov, S. (1987). Congressional perceptions of the elderly: The use of stereotypes in the legislative process. *The Gerontologist, 27,* 77–78.

The author analyzed the content of 893 speeches given in Congress and found numerous occurrences of ageist stereotypes. This article is recommended for students, faculty, and professionals with an interest in social policy.

Chapter 8: Moving to a Long-Term Care Facility

Breckman, R., & Adelman, R. (1988). *Strategies for helping victims of elder mistreatment.* Newbury Park, CA: Sage Publications.

This excellent book includes key chapters on definitions, detection, assessment, and intervention. The text should prove highly useful to both practitioners and educators.

Heiselman, T., & Noelker, L. (1991). Enhancing mutual respect among nursing assistants, residents, and residents' families. *The Gerontologist, 31,* 552–555.

This small study of 40 nursing assistants and 37 residents gave rise to an in-service session on interpersonal respect. In-service educators and nursing managers may benefit from this article.

Lincoln Medical Education Foundation. (1990). *Resident's bill of rights* (video, ¹/₂" VHS, 20 minutes). Lincoln, NE.

This videotape examines the rights of residents in nursing homes. It focuses on facilitating maximum freedom of choice for residents. Responsibilities of the staff in protecting resident rights are addressed.

Mikhail, M. (1992). Psychological responses to relocation to a nursing home. *Journal of Gerontological Nursing, 18*(3), 35–39.

This article reviews factors that influence psychological responses and adaptation to relocation to a nursing home. The author concludes that a central theme in psychological responses is the resident's perception of how much control the resident will have over their life.

Pillemer, K., & Moore, D. (1989). Abuse of patients in nursing homes: Findings from a survey of staff. *The Gerontologist, 29,* 314–320.

Pillemer and Moore report on a telephone survey of nurses and nursing aides. Characteristics of abusive staff are described.

Video Press, University of Maryland. (1991). *Transitions* (video, ¹/₂" VHS, 20 minutes). Baltimore: University of Maryland.

This videotape addresses the planning and preparation essential before relocation, a change of living arrangements, or institutionalization. Health professionals discuss facilitation techniques for dealing with stress for both the family and the older person.

Chapter 9: Death and Dying

Butler, R. (1963). The life review: An interpretation of reminiscence in the aged. *Psychiatry, 26,* 65–76.

This classic paper explains the importance of life review as an integrative process. It is a "must read" for professionals interacting with older adults.

Cameron, P., Stewart, L., & Biber, H. (1973). Consciousness of death across the life span. *Journal of Gerontology, 28,* 92–95.

This paper covers an empirical study on preoccupation with thoughts of death. It is recommended for graduate students and faculty.

Glick, I., Weiss, R., & Parkes, C. (1974). *The first year of bereavement.* New York: John Wiley & Sons.

Although this study, based upon interviews of young widows, is somewhat dated, it sheds much light on the bereavement process.

Haight, B. (1991). Reminiscing: The state of the art as a basis for practice. *International Journal of Aging and Human Development, 33,* 1–32.

Haight provides a thorough review of 30 years of research on rem-

iniscence and life review. This paper is recommended for faculty in nursing, social work, and geropsychology.

Kalish, R. (1981). *Death, grief, and caring relationships.* Monterey, CA: Brooks/Cole.

Kalish, one of the leaders of the death education movement, mixes compassion with clear reporting of behavioral science research. This is a very useful reference text.

Leviton, D. (1986–87). Thanatological theory and my dying father. *Omega, 17,* 127–144.

This beautifully written paper describes how the author and his father prepared psychologically for the latter's death. Several theories of dying are described and applied. The article should prove valuable for faculty, students, and professionals working with older adults.

Nicholl, G. (1984–85). The life review in five short stories about characters facing death. *Omega, 15,* 85–96.

The author analyzes the role of life review in short fiction by Leo Tolstoy, Ernest Hemingway, Katherine Anne Porter, Willa Cather, and Tillie Olsen. Readers interested in life review will find this article interesting.

Paradis, L. (Ed.). (1985). *Hospice handbook: A guide for managers and planners.* Rockville, MD: Aspen.

This handbook covers a wide range of issues regarding hospices. This book should prove useful to health care educators and practitioners.

Chapter 10: Issues for Professional Caregivers

Applebaum, S. (1980). *Stress management for health care professionals.* Rockville, MD: Aspen.

Though somewhat dated, this book includes valuable material on stress in healthcare organizations, effects of stress on the family, troubled employees, and conflict management. Six useful cases are presented at the end of the text.

Drury, S. (1984). *Assertive supervision: Building involved teamwork.* Champaign, IL: Research Press.

This clearly written guidebook offers the supervisor workable tactics for dealing with the competing demands of administrative work. A series of practical exercises is included. This book is recommended to both administrative staff and educators.

Giordano, J., & Backham, K. (1985). The aged within a family context: Relationships, roles and events. In L. L'Abate (Ed.), *The handbook of family psychology and therapy* (Vol. 1, pp. 284–320). Homewood, IL: Dorsey Press.

This chapter surveys the issues facing the aging family. Especially useful is the section on the dysfunctional family. Written in a scholarly style, this material should prove valuable to faculty and graduate students.

Girdano, D., & Everly, G. (1986). *Controlling stress and tension: A holistic approach.* Englewood Cliffs, NJ: Prentice-Hall.

Using an interdisciplinary approach, Girdano and Everly present strategies for managing everyday stress. Included is a very readable section on the physiology of stress that could prove helpful to health educators in the preparation of presentations on stress and stress management.

Greenberg, J. (1990). *Comprehensive stress management* (3rd ed.). Dubuque, IA: William C. Brown.

Designed for undergraduate courses in health education and psychology, this book is a real gem. Anyone contemplating the development of a workshop or course on the topic should find much usable content and a host of learner exercises. There are strong sections on assertiveness, meditation, progressive relaxation, exercise, occupational stress (including burnout) and stress and older adults.

Kermis, M. (1986). *Mental health in later life: The adaptive process.* Monterey, CA: Jones and Bartlett.

This textbook offers valuable information for the health care practitioner and educator confronted with the mental health needs of older clients. There are very fine chapters on stress, value dilemmas for the professional, diagnosis and assessment, and functional disorders.

Lazarus, R., & DeLongis, A. (1983). Psychological stress and coping in aging, *American Psychologist, 38,* 245–254.

This highly academic article examines the role of "hassles" and "uplifts" in the lives of older adults. This article is recommended for faculty, graduate students, and advanced undergraduates.

WGBH-TV. (1986). *Stress to your advantage* (video, VHS, 30 minutes). Boston.

This videotape shows the viewer how to adapt to the distressors of daily life.

Notes

Notes

Notes

Notes

Notes

Notes

Notes

Notes

Notes

Notes

Notes

Notes